HOW
TO
BUILD
A
FAMILY

HOW TO BUILD A FAMILY

KATE FERDINAND

Vermilion, an imprint of Ebury Publishing
20 Vauxhall Bridge Road
London SW1V 2SA

Vermilion is part of the Penguin Random House group of companies
whose addresses can be found at global.penguinrandomhouse.com

Copyright © Kate Ferdinand 2023
Illustrations by Emily Voller

First published by Vermilion in 2023

www.penguin.co.uk

A CIP catalogue record for this book is available from the British Library

ISBN 9781785044076

Printed and bound in Great Britain by Clays Ltd, Elcograf S.p.A.
The authorised representative in the EEA is Penguin Random House
Ireland, Morrison Chambers, 32 Nassau Street, Dublin D02 YH68

Penguin Random House is committed to a sustainable future for
our business, our readers and our planet. This book is made from
Forest Stewardship Council® certified paper.

For Lorenz, Tate, Tia and Cree.
Be unapologetically you; you're perfect as you are.

CONTENTS

INTRODUCTION

Hi, I'm Kate. Stepmum to Lorenz, Tate and Tia. Mum to Cree. Dog mum to Ronnie. And wife to Rio. I'm called 'Mummy', 'Kate' and 'Mummy Kate' in our house, but I'll explain all that later.

I was 26 when I met Rio on the beach while on holiday. I was young, free and single, and living my best life. Rio, on the other hand, was 38, with three kids and widowed – the perfect match! Lol. It wasn't exactly what I wanted to go home and tell my mum about and it certainly wasn't what I'd imagined when I'd envisaged my future family, but you can't control how you feel. And I didn't anticipate just how strong my bond with Rio would be.

When I fell in love with Rio, it all seemed pretty simple to me, at first. I thought, 'How could I love this man without loving his whole life and everything that is his?' I never questioned it. 'If they're his children and he loves them, well, then I'll love them too. And I'll make it work, because we're one.' Sorted. If only it were that simple!

When I look back to that time, it feels like worlds away and I can see now that I was naïve. I didn't know what I was getting into and I had no idea how much time and effort it would take to create a fully blended family. Yet there's a lot to be said for feeling optimistic and full of hope as you head out on this journey – start as you mean to go on, I say!

Although sometimes our life may look perfect from the outside, I can assure you it's not. I'm so grateful now for my big blended family, and the bumps in the road aren't coming so often these days, but it's been one hell of a journey to get here.

Every family takes hard work, time, love and attention, but a blended family needs that little bit extra and I truly believe that our love is so deep because of everything we've been through as a couple and as a family. Where in the early days I'd feel worried about using the word 'family' as people would judge me, I can sit here confidently now and say that we *are* a family and I'm proud of where we are today. We've really fought and worked for this, which makes it extra special.

Isn't it funny how some of our greatest struggles bring us on to the greatest moments in life? Without those lows we wouldn't appreciate the highs.

WHY THIS BOOK?

Becoming part of a blended family, whether through a break-up, fostering, adopting or a loss, brings so much happiness and joy, and is so fulfilling, but there's no getting away from the fact that it can also be tricky and emotional when you're trying to navigate unknown territory.

I searched high and low for a how-to guide to my situation when I started out, but while bookshops and websites are full of parenting books, the stepparenting sections are tiny and the handbook I was looking for didn't seem to exist. This book has been in the making for a while – I just started jotting down notes and ideas, one thing led to another, and now you're reading it!

I struggled with being a stepmum in the beginning, partly because I had no one to share my experiences with and felt that no one understood what I was going through. The first years were the hardest and I wanted reassurance that things would get easier; I had a lot of self-doubt and needed to know that people in my situation were facing the same challenges as I was. Eventually, my longing to reach out to other stepparents inspired me to set up Blended and, without this community and the support it offers me, I would still feel very alone.

Looking after children who have lost a parent brings its own set of challenges and, while it's amazing, it can also be challenging. It's been a real journey for me and I've pretty much been learning on the job – and winging it most of the time! – but one thing I have realised is that the more we share our experiences, the less alone we feel. I've found that there is power in sharing your struggles to help others.

Don't get me wrong, I still have my wobbles, which is why I feel it's so important to connect with you all – I want to widen that community and reach anyone who needs support. My *Blended* podcast has also really supported me in my journey, leading me into in-depth discussions with both experts and everyday people on everything from second marriages and divorce to life after loss and (not-so-wicked!) stepmothers. Over the last few years I've realised just how important it is for someone to be out there championing the different voices and experiences of stepparents and their families. There was a real lack of this when I was just starting out on my journey. I'm passionate about connecting people who are trying to build a new family structure. It goes without saying that we can all help each other – and this book is an extension of that.

I'm not going to pretend I have all the answers. Every blended family is blended differently, so that would be impossible. But I will say that if you can just stick with it through the downs as well as the ups, being a step- or bonus parent may well turn out to be one of the most rewarding things you ever do. Sometimes it's difficult – especially when your feelings are all over the place and you can't make head nor tail of what's going on – but if your intentions are pure and you're coming from a place of love, I believe that the pieces of the jigsaw will eventually fall into place.

Here you'll find some of the lessons I've learned along the way, the tips and hints I wish I'd known and answers to the questions I've been asked, if I know them, as well as advice and guidance from experts for when things go wrong. I will be talking to chartered psychologist, author and founder of Happy Steps, Professor Lisa Doodson, throughout the book, as well as Louise Allen, bestselling author and campaigner for children in care; Laura Herman, psychotherapist, school counsellor and co-founder of Thinking-Together about Parenting Teens; Anna Mathur, psychotherapist, bestselling author and podcaster; Laura Naser, award-winning family lawyer and author; Sophie Rantzau, counsellor to families and stepfamilies, and stepmum of three; Julia Samuel, MBE, psychotherapist, author and podcaster; Dr Emma Svanberg, award-winning clinical psychologist and author; Carly Keen, founder of EQ Essex, and Dr Dominique Thompson, award-winning mental health expert, former university GP and author. I'm so grateful to all these experts and contributors who have offered their words of wisdom.

I also feel incredibly lucky to have met so many wonderful blended families over the last few years and I wanted to bring those voices into the book too so as many of you feel represented as possible. You'll come across stories and experiences from other stepparents from the Blended community throughout the book, helping to shine a light on the different dilemmas many families face. I've also turned to the Blended community for examples of situations I haven't personally experienced. It's in these accounts where you'll find the real stepparenting wisdom that we all long for – and it's coming from the people who have lived it and got the T-shirt. I hope you'll find it helpful to hear their experiences in their own words. I'm so grateful to them for their generous contributions.

The fact that 'family' can mean different things to different people definitely needs wider acceptance. By sharing how we're dealing with challenges across the spectrum, we can help each other get over all kinds of obstacles. I'm aware that I'm just one voice: in my house, I love the kids, and I feel that they love me, and I don't really have that fight over whether or not I'm their real mum. But I know there are lots of people who do have that struggle, and a host of other issues, and I also know that I'm faced with difficulties that other people seem to breeze through.

Having said that, there are some common themes and concerns around being a stepparent that seem to crop up again and again – both on the podcast and Instagram – and I've tried to cover as many of these as possible in the book, including:

» dealing with grief and divorce

» wondering if the kids will like and accept you

» comparison to previous partners

» how to move into the family home and start making changes

» concerns about disrupting the routine of the home and finding your own way

» building relationships with the wider family

You know what? It's worth being ambitious about what you can achieve with love and hard work. I'm here to tell you that, as a stepparent, you can be a really positive addition to the family you are joining: you can be a force for good and a fantastic role model. You *can* build a happy, blended family.

The aim of this book is to encourage and inspire, comfort and support stepparents and families everywhere. I want this book to help you feel less alone and more empowered. Although I don't have the experience of other blended set-ups, such as fostering or adoption, and these are such big subjects in themselves that it would be impossible to do them justice in this book, I really hope that, whatever your family arrangement may look like, this will be your go-to reference as you experience the joys – and challenges – of the blended experience. Because whoever you are and whatever your situation, just by taking on this challenge, you are amazing.

CHAPTER 1

WHAT IT
MEANS TO BE
A STEPPARENT

*'A family doesn't have to be
normal to be special'*

Most of us don't grow up thinking we'll become stepparents. I know I didn't. In fact, if someone had told me that one day I'd be somebody's stepmum, I honestly don't think I'd have believed them. In my mind, I was the last person on earth to take on that role because my number one thing was that I would never go out with a man who had children. When my friends went out with men with kids, I'd be like, 'No way, I'd never do that!'

I'm still not sure why I felt so strongly about this, especially coming from a broken-up family myself. For some reason, growing up, I always assumed that I'd get married, we'd have our own children and that would be that. I just didn't question it, despite my own childhood experience, and I think it says quite a lot about the power of social norms that I fully expected to create a nuclear family, when an estimated one in three families in the UK are part of the blended experience.*

If you're anything like me, you might find it hard to let go of your original idea of what happily ever after would look like for you. And that's OK – just as it's OK to feel intimidated by what you're taking on and how much responsibility joining an already-made family will mean for you.

Now I'm older, I know that life has a way of surprising us. It can be challenging when things don't pan out the way you imagined, but I'm a strong believer that everything happens for a reason and I wouldn't now have it any other way.

Stepparenting situations vary massively and where you fit in will largely depend on your individual family's circumstances. Blending a family with young children is going to be very different from blending teens, children of assorted ages or grown-ups. A lot depends on whether the previous partner is involved – or is absent, friendly or hostile.

In this chapter, we'll explore the different types of blended homes, your role as a stepparent, the importance of your relationship with your partner, meeting the stepchildren as well as tips on how to prepare for blended family life. It really helps to have the common interest of doing the best for the children and using that as a base to work around. The happiness of the children and the home as a whole are the most important things.

Going by my own experience, I am here because, well, I fell madly in love with Rio – that all-consuming love, where

---

* Sherwood, H., 17 Aug. 2021. 'Goodbye wicked stepmother: "bonus" families adopting more positive terms'. *Guardian*. Retrieved from https://wwwtheguardian.com/uk-news/2021/aug/17/goodbye-wicked-stepmother-bonus-families-adopting-more-positive-terms.

I wanted to spend the rest of my life with him. So, naturally, that meant loving and caring for his children too.

I was still in *The Only Way Is Essex* (*TOWIE*) when I met Rio – gosh, that feels like a lifetime ago – but once things became serious, we soon realised that *TOWIE* life wouldn't be the best fit for the family. Rio's kids needed support and stability, and I could tell that they were lacking someone in a motherly role; I wanted to give them what they were missing from their mum.

I didn't realise how many factors and emotions would be involved or how deep it all went. I didn't foresee the emotional turmoil and difficulties ahead. But I really, really wanted to make it work because I loved Rio and believed that we could all have a happy future together.

Several years down the line, I can honestly say that I feel confident in my role as the children's stepmum. I have a wonderful husband, the kids are fantastic and we've worked hard to create a happy, blended unit. There's no doubt in my mind that being part of this family is a blessing.

It hasn't always been easy, though. Whatever life or route you take, there are always going to be struggles in a family. Things might look perfect through the lens of social media, but everyone has their difficult moments. Being a stepparent is complicated – emotionally and in ways you won't have even thought of until you get here – and, like so many of the best things in life, you have to put in the effort to make it work.

But it's not all negative – there are so many positive things that come with being a stepparent. It just takes time, love, care and patience for those positives to shine through. And, trust me, once you've worked for the love, when you get the rewards, they feel even better.

Remember, you and your partner are here because you have fallen in love and decided to share your lives. Doesn't that just show the power of love?

'There is nothing love cannot face; there is no limit to its faith, its hope and its endurance ... In a word, there are three things that last forever: faith, hope and love; but the greatest of them all is love.'

THE BIBLE, 1 CORINTHIANS 13

> *I always wanted a 'normal' family. I never wanted to meet someone with children. I always wanted to give my partner their first child. Whether that was down to how people look at it from the outside, or because the 2.4 family was perceived as perfect, or I worried about the stigma, I just don't know. Now I'm so glad things happened differently. Blending is challenging, but so rewarding, because you're giving and receiving love that isn't automatic.*
>
> DANIELLE, BLENDED FAMILY OF THREE

WHAT DOES A BLENDED FAMILY LOOK LIKE?

Being part of a blended family is still very much unknown territory and social acceptance is not on the side of stepparents, especially if you're a stepmother, and that's partly the fault of a bunch of outdated fairy tales.

One lady I met told me that her stepson had come home from school one day and told her she was wicked. 'Why, what have I done?' she asked him.

'Stepmothers are evil,' he said, 'and you're my stepmother.'

History and literature haven't given us much to go by. Fairy tales and historical texts are full of cruel, vindictive 'step-monsters'. Stepmothers in particular seem to have an unfairly bad reputation, when the reality is that it takes a really strong person to be a stepparent.

It's extremely unhelpful for the modern stepmum (as she puts on the fifth wash of the day and rushes to get her stepkids to school) that some of the very first stories we're told as kids paint stepmothers as cruel and self-interested. These tales date from hundreds of years ago, when life was harsh and women were very much second-class citizens. Second wives were common because so many mothers died in childbirth, but they were viewed with suspicion. Without a biological link, people wondered, without a natural mater-nal instinct, why would you go the extra mile for someone else's kids? Love for a partner was clearly not seen as a good enough reason!

We've come a long way, thankfully – and yet these nega-tive myths keep being repeated to each new generation. It may be that they're serving a collective purpose – as cautionary tales to kids to beware of strangers or a lesson in the evils of humanity – and yet they're very unfair to stepmothers. No one is writing grisly folk tales about stepdads, perhaps because men are still seen as protectors and providers, above all else. Let's change the narrative – not all stepmums are evil.

Whatever your situation and whether you already have kids or not (and if you do, that brings with it a whole new set of logistics), becoming a stepparent is like starting a new job – with no one to teach you and no mentor to guide you. You've just got to figure it all out on your own. I came into this situation as a childless stepmum (I don't love that phrase, but how else do you describe it!). Now that I've had Cree (my biological son), I've realised how difficult it was in those early days. I didn't know anything about the practicalities of looking after children – like what time they're meant to have dinner or when they need to have a bath – and felt really out of my depth. Although I'm quite maternal, I had no young children in the family and so no experience of what was required. The love came instantly, but the practical side took a while to get my head around. I just wasn't prepared for that parenting role.

Each blended family is unique and your set-up may be very different to mine, but whatever your access and however much you see the children, always remember that you are a parent.

Things can get really tough at times, which is why you need to know that just by trying to make it work, you are doing something amazing.

'Biological, step, foster, adoptive. It's not the word before 'parent' that defines you, but rather the love and commitment in your heart.'

DIFFERENT TYPES OF HOMES

This section might sound really simple and like I'm stating the obvious, but when you're in a new situation, it's sometimes helpful to see things written down in black and white, so let's go through the different blended family set-ups. Once you've figured out what set-up you're in, you can start the process of figuring out what you need to do next. That's one thing crossed off the list!

The full-time home

I'll start with me. I became a full-time stepmum and moved into the family home, which meant it went from zero to one hundred real quick!

The huge bonus of living full-time with your blended family is that you have much more of a chance to become close and bond into a single unit. I love my stepchildren and I'm glad we're together all the time, but being a full-time stepparent does mean that you don't get a lot of time off from the children to focus on your partner.

Since your relationship hasn't included those early child-free years, when couples typically have fewer responsibilities and worries, it's especially important that you have the chance to enjoy time together apart from the kids. Even if it's just sitting down for a meal in a separate room while the children watch a film together, you need time and space to enjoy each other (see page 113 for more tips on how to create moments of connection with your partner).

I'm lucky to be in a situation where my stepchildren accept me, so I never have a sense of feeling unwanted in my own home, but I know that isn't the case for everyone.

The majority-time home

This is where the home is the children's main base and contact with the non-resident parent is limited to weekends and holidays.

If you live for the majority of the time with your own children from a previous relationship as well as your stepchildren, you probably feel your time and love is being stretched to the limit, and finances could also be tight.

Use the times when your stepchildren visit the non-resident parent to strengthen ties with the family remaining in the home – whether that's your biological children or your partner – and to recharge your energy levels. If possible, arrange schedules so that you and your partner get to have time just the two of you, at least every now and then.

Plan as much as you can. Try to co-ordinate timings and visits to suit everybody's needs and purposes. There are all kinds of apps to help you organise the home and your schedule (see pages 219–20), and it also might be a good idea to print out a planner and put it on the wall for everybody to see (see the family planner on pages 16–17). It can be reassuring for all ages to know what's happening in the coming days and weeks.

Putting the children first means finding the best set-up for them. Most children thrive when they are in close contact with both parents, although they may not realise it at the time (and you may not, either!).

The shared-access home

If you're sharing 50:50 access, some or all of the children in your family will be spending half their time with at least one other parent, and your home and family unit will expand and contract accordingly. This can play out in different ways: collaboration and co-operation; a tendency to compare or contrast lifestyles or approaches to parenting; and there may also be a competitive element or, sadly, open hostility.

It's easy to think of your home as being the children's 'real' base and the place they go to visit the non-resident parent as being more temporary. But the children may see both places as home, even if they spend less time in one than the other.

Equally, if they don't visit you very often or if their visiting patterns aren't set and predictable, they may not actually feel very secure in your home. Feelings about home(s) can get very complicated for children, who crave continuity and a sense of belonging and ease.

Alternatively, they may feel like outsiders at the non-resident parent's home, if there are step- or half-siblings living there full-time or if the other siblings aren't there when they visit. It's not unusual for kids to feel jealous of step- and half-siblings, or to feel overlooked or loved less. Anything that gives them a sense of being excluded from a core family unit will undermine their sense of home.

You can help them to feel at home in more than one place. Even if you can't affect how they feel when they're staying with their other parent, you can make sure they know they belong in your home. Ideally, they need to feel welcome when they arrive and slot into the rhythm of whichever base they find themselves in. After you've greeted them and offered them something to eat or drink, it might help to update them on events coming up and discuss any needs they might have going forward. (See Chapter 4 for more ideas on bonding as a family and pages 21–2 for tips on helping children transition between homes.)

Guilt eats us away as parents. Professor Lisa Doodson has some tips on ensuring your bio child feels included and equally cared for and loved if they spend 50 per cent of their time away from the home (page 18).

Weekly Family Planner

MON

TUE

WED

THU

FRI

SAT

SUN

DON'T FORGET

MUST DOS

THINGS FOR NEXT WEEK

HELPING CHILDREN TO SETTLE INTO A SHARED-ACCESS ROUTE

PROFESSOR LISA DOODSON

» It's really common for bio parents to feel guilty when they have to share their children with their ex-partner, but your child is more than likely absolutely fine when in their other parent's home. These feelings will subside over time once you've all settled into a new routine.

» Make sure you have 'parent and child time' when your bio child comes to visit. Find something to do together every time you see them. Make this your special time together.

» Don't be tempted to treat your bio child differently to other children in the home. If you treat all the children the same, it'll help your child feel truly part of the family unit and improve their relationship with any other children in the home.

» Children are always better off spending time with both their bio parents (assuming there is no history of harm or abuse), so while you and your ex may parent differently, remind yourself that your child is loved and well cared for when they are with their other bio parent.

» When your child isn't with you, remember you *are* allowed to have a good time! You aren't being disloyal to your child.

» Concentrate on giving love, affection and time to your child/children when they're with you, not showering them with gifts or treats. It's about creating a normal home life for them, where they'll feel happy and safe.

I met my partner of nine years through a mutual friend. His wife had died and our three boys went to the same primary school. Fast forward a few years and we now have three strapping teenagers! Unfortunately we don't live together as yet, even though we would love to live as a family – it's the problem of moving and buying and fear of upsetting the kids. It's OK and we have got used to things the way they are. However, it's funny how everyone else seems to have a problem with it! I'm always asked why we don't live together, why we are not married, the kids would just have to accept it, it's your lives too ... People who are not in our situation just don't understand the enormity of children losing a mother when they're still so young. Of course we would love to all be together, but it works and our three boys are well-behaved, decent and hard-working kids. We would like to think that we as parents have made them this way!

LOU, BLENDED FAMILY OF FIVE

The weekend home

You might be blending at weekends, which could mean it will take a bit longer to get to know the kids and build bonds with them, but then again … maybe it won't! Every family set-up is unique.

There are positives and negatives to being a stepparent only at weekends. It can be easier than having the children the majority of the time, because the time you have with them is time off with less pressure and more emphasis on fun. On the flip side, if you mainly have the children during the week, it can feel like all work and no play, which can impact your relationship with them. Try to balance things out if you can.

SCHEDULING FOR SUCCESS
PROFESSOR LISA DOODSON

If you are new as a stepfamily and are still trying to make sense of it, a bit of planning works wonders. If you can make a plan and, say, split a weekend into different parts, you're setting expectations of how the weekend will look. Find time for you all to do something together and make memories, as well as time for bio parents to spend with their children on their own. If you're the stepparent and are feeling overwhelmed, add in a bit of time when you're on your own and can re-energise and refresh. Don't feel guilty about doing this – everybody needs a bit of time to reset.

Tips on transitioning between homes

For children, it can throw up emotional issues to transition from one parent's home to another. It may be a jolting reminder that the family has broken up, or trigger memories of the unhappy break-up, or the time leading up to it.

If you're a stepparent in a 50:50 shared access home or you have some or all of the children at weekends, it can really help if you and your partner have a plan to help the children transition from one home to the other without too much upset or disruption. The following tips might help:

» Try listening to music or an audiobook on the journey.

» Stop off at a playground or a sweet shop, or pop in and see Granny. If the kids associate the transition with something fun or positive, they are much more likely to accept that it needs to happen.

» Praise them for helping when it goes well. If it doesn't, acknowledge it and ask them how they think it could have gone better.

» If there's any chance of the transition becoming tricky, it's a good idea to do pick-ups and drop offs in a public place – a playground, an ice cream parlour or a shopping mall; somewhere convenient for you where your child is happy to go, depending on their age. This can be the best solution even if the adults get on well.

> » If you have a court order for access and your previous partner is at all difficult, do the handover in a public place and take along a friend or close relative to smooth the transition and to record timings and behaviour, if necessary.
>
> » If a child's bio parents disagree about contact, it can take place at – or children can be dropped off and collected from – a Child Contact Centre near you.

My stepson Alfie struggles with anxiety and found the transition between his mum's household and his dad's very difficult at first. This was heartbreaking to see, especially for his mum, Zoe. However, she was very supportive and we all agreed to persevere, as Alfie would settle very quickly and have a great time, and we all knew how important it was for him to have this time with his dad.

When Alfie was with us, we ensured he had a consistent routine, as it relieves his anxiety when he knows what is happening and when. We would also reassure Alfie whenever he seemed to be getting anxious, either by talking to him or allowing him to speak to his mum if he needed to. We have tried to have a consistent approach between households, which has helped. Alfie's dad also made sure he spent time pursuing topics that Alfie was interested in, giving them valuable time together.

We have come out of the other side with Alfie. It took a year for him to truly start to settle properly without any major anxiety. He now freely comes and goes and looks forward to family holidays, even if it means he is away from his mum longer than usual. At the height of Alfie's anxiety, I never thought we would get to this stage.

It has only been possible to do all of this because Alfie's mum is open to working with us without criticism or negativity. When issues arise, we discuss them openly between the adults, which has allowed the children to feel safe and secure whether they are at our home or at their own.

TONI, BLENDED FAMILY OF EIGHT

Keep in mind that, no matter what your set-up looks like, there will be a settling-in period that can last months or even years, and your role will probably change over time, as you grow closer to the children.

YOUR ROLE

As the stepparent coming into an already-made family, you don't really have a position. Who are you? What is your role? I know how hard it is to find your feet.

In the early days, I used to look at my friends on social media – with their partners and kids – and feel really envious. It all looked so easy and 'normal'. Even when I'd hear the kids call my friends 'Mum' or 'Dad', I longed for it to be that simple for us. It's much more complex being a stepparent and, when you haven't yet figured out how it works for you as a family, other people are on edge around you too. Believe me, though, once it all falls into place, it's much clearer. I'm now confident with my role in the family.

For me, it was very important to acknowledge that I would never take the role of Rebecca – the children's biological mum – but I believe that all three of us (me, Rio and Rebecca) have contributed to bringing the kids up and making them who they are today.

It's often helpful to tell yourself, right from the start, that even though you're not the biological parent, you can be another, equally important, parent.

On paper, I think I'm pretty well suited to being a step-mum. I still doubt myself all the time, though! Most stepparents do, I think. In fact, most *parents* do. And it's probably quite a healthy feeling, as long as it doesn't get in the way too much.

In my favour, I'm naturally a very caring person and I've always had the desire to look after people. If I see someone unhappy, I make it my mission to try to cheer them up. My parents split when I was very young and I can empathise with feeling lonely or sad; when I was a kid, I longed for the love that I'm giving now and I'm glad that I can make a difference.

Is being caring enough, though? Do you need any special qualities?

This is a hard one. More than anything, I'm tempted to say, 'Patience, patience, patience!' and leave it at that. I still struggle with this one, though – at times, I have no patience at all! I'm talking about anything from asking the children ten times to clean their teeth in an evening or getting them to sit down to do their homework. (In fact, now that I think about it, I'm not sure the kids listen to me at all!)

In my experience, there are some things I've had to draw on when it comes to parenting. To be clear, though, I don't always manage them!

1. **Love** is the foundation of everything, especially parenting. If in doubt, don't overthink things: this is the one that counts.

2. **Patience** …This is a big ask when you've got kids pulling and pushing you in different directions and people judging you, all mixed in with wondering whether you're doing the right thing. You'd have to be totally zen not to become annoyed or anxious at times within a blended family – there are so many challenges along the way – and so patience is probably a quality you're learning to *work towards*; something you want, can't always have, but keep on trying for.

3. **Empathy** is putting yourself in somebody else's shoes and responding to them emotionally. It is about opening your heart to people and being intuitive about their feelings; it's about joining the dots between experience, behaviour and emotion. Having empathy will help you put your own ego aside and lead to a kinder, more compassionate approach to loving and parenting.

4. **Adaptability** is important, because things don't always go as planned and new challenges appear all the time when you're building a family. If you're flexible and adaptable, you can respond, react and go with the flow.

None of us have got this sussed, but if you can try your best to tap into these qualities, the journey may feel lighter. Many times, I've felt like I've been lacking in a lot of these and to continue feels like the hardest thing. That's when you need to remind yourself of who you really are – and who you want to be going forward; this will make all the difference to what sort of parent you will be.

As you'll see throughout the book, it's taken me time to be comfortable with my position as a stepmum – and it's meant I've had to put other people's opinions to one side and brush off the inevitable comparisons. Now I'm fully comfortable in my position as a wife and stepparent, I find this easier, and I know that, in time, you will too.

YOU AND YOUR PARTNER ARE THE FOUNDATION

Being a stepparent can be really difficult at times, so I am thankful that Rio and I have such a good relationship. We've been through a lot together – sometimes it feels as if, in just a few years, we've been through what some couples go through during 10 or 15. For us, it was toughest at the beginning. Helping the kids to navigate bereavement was – and still is – a big challenge, and we'll explore this in more detail in the next chapter. There was a lot going on emotionally – dealing with the comparison to a previous wife as well as trying to build a new family and give the children love and a sense of security – and it put a lot of pressure on our relationship. However, for me and Rio, dealing with difficult issues has only strengthened the bond between us. I knew deep down that somehow we'd find a balance and make things work.

The importance of shared values

You and your partner may be very different, but ideally you'll have a shared vision for your family. It's OK if one of you is a frugal vegetarian atheist and the other loves shopping, steak and spiritual retreats, as long as you can broadly agree on what is best for your family and future. It also helps if you see eye to eye when it comes to family values because shared values give your new unit a sense of identity and stability.

It's taken a while, but Rio and I have set the following values for our family – we've found them really helpful and it means we're all on the same page. They've helped us find a level of respect for each other and, as a result, it means that – mostly! – our family life runs more smoothly.

Don't get me wrong – this takes time. You're not going to get there overnight, but I hope seeing how we've shaped our values might help as a starting point:

» Number one for our family is honesty – for us it's important to be honest about all things … from the little things, like who left their dirty plate on the kitchen counter, to the bigger things, like how we feel about our emotions.

» Another value for us is communication. With clear communication we can help each other more. If someone is having a bad day, you can understand it if you all just communicate.

» Being respectful is a big one for me. Respect takes a long time to gain, especially when you're forming a blended family.

» Be you: when I think about all my kids – as well as me and Rio – I just want them to have the confidence to be themselves without any judgement. In the early months, I tried to be everything that everyone wanted me to be (more on that later!) rather than be myself. Once I started to be myself, everything fell into place a little bit more.

» Have fun. All of the above values are important, but having fun and creating memories is what it's really all about.

Let me just add here that I'm saying this after six years of being a stepmum. In the first year, I don't think we had any of these sussed – and especially not all at once. Lol!

IS THERE A RIGHT TIME TO MEET THE CHILDREN?

What a loaded question! There's a lot of debate on parenting websites about how and when to introduce kids to a new partner. Most people seem to think that you should wait at least six months before introducing a potential stepparent; others say you should follow your instinct and just do what feels right. I've read advice suggesting that it's not a good look to be dating different people openly in front of the kids. But one mum argued that being a single parent is actually a great chance to model healthy dating and romance to your children. We're all different – and so are our kids – so what's the best way to approach this?

If you're a potential stepparent coming into an already-made family, you should be aware of how much biological parents worry about their children's feelings in this situation, especially how they will cope if they get attached to a new partner and the relationship doesn't work out. Obviously, parents will have to be the judge of how sensitive their kids are and what is best for them. They should also be prepared to guide the new partner coming in.

INTRODUCING A NEW PARTNER TO THE KIDS

LAURA NASER

The general advice is that a new partner should not be introduced to children unless the relationship has longevity and a permanence to it. There is no hard and fast rule about what this actually means for a relationship because they can all develop differently and have different intentions. For example, you might have a close friendship for many years prior to it becoming a relationship, in which case you may feel more sure of your joint intentions and may be able to safely introduce that person to your children earlier than you would if you had just met that person prior to dating.

The risks are that you do not want anyone you cannot truly trust to be around your children, and you also don't want your children to become attached to a new significant person in their life if you are not sure that they will be staying around. While it is beneficial to speak to your co-parent about the introduction of a new partner to your children in advance, it is not always going to be appropriate. You will need to make a decision based on how you anticipate their reaction might be and approach the topic carefully with that in mind.

There is plenty of guidance available online about this topic, but from a legal perspective, it's about making sure the decision is being done with your children's best interests at the forefront of your mind. No two children are the same and so I recommend that you reflect upon

> their experience to date, their own levels of maturity and understanding, and their wishes and feelings on the topic in addition to making sure the relationship is stable.

Waiting until you're really sure the relationship is going somewhere before meeting or introducing the children makes sense to me. I worry that it could be disruptive and destabilising for them to meet and then lose a potential stepparent. But a post I read by a mum blogger said the opposite. She felt that children are used to people coming and going in their lives: relatives move away, best friends split up and go to different schools and teachers change classes every year. In other words, she doesn't think it's a big deal.

Every situation is different, but perhaps it's worth thinking about how you both present the new relationship to the kids in the first place.

There is no right or wrong way, but Rio and I decided it was best to meet at a friend's house and that I would bring my little dog, Ronnie, along as a way to bond with the children.

I met the kids four months after meeting Rio. Initially, I was introduced to them in a non-romantic way as a friend of a friend. But that doesn't mean I wasn't terrified when I first met them! All sorts of questions were running through my mind:

» Are the kids going to like me?

» Do they want me here?

» Am I going to get on with them?

I've still got the selfie I took of me and Ronnie in the car on the way to meet Lorenz, Tate and Tia for the first time. I remember that day so clearly; I was desperate for the children to like me. They had no clue who I was, but they loved dogs; they chased Ronnie around the garden and put him in a little trolley and pushed him around.

Then Rio gave me his jumper, because it was cold, and one of them said in surprise, 'Look, Dad's just given that girl his jumper!' Once the children got used to seeing my face, it all developed quite naturally from there.

What the children might worry about when they meet a potential stepparent

» Why are you here?

» Are you going to take my dad/mum away?

» Will you get in the way or mess up our relationship?

» Does Mum love you more than she loves/loved Dad?

» Did my family split up because of you?

» Are you the reason my other parent is unhappy?

» Will my other parent mind if I like you?

» Are you really strict?/Are you going to change everything?

» Do you like me?

» Are you going to be mean to me?

What they might be hoping for

» Will you make Dad/Mum/us happy again?

» Will you make us feel secure again?

» Will we be a happy family again?

» Will you get us to school on time?

» Will you cook the sort of food I like eating?

All of these are valid feelings, but, in time, the more your relationship grows, the more the kids will feel secure and see you as less of a threat.

It's worth giving some reassurance to the children. In the early days, I would always say to the kids, 'I'm not here to replace Mummy.' It's about building your own relationship with them with your own experiences and memories, which we'll discuss in Chapter 4.

I was introduced to Alfie as 'Daddy's friend' and it was done at a friend's house, on completely neutral ground. We spent some time alone and I just asked him what he was playing and he came over and showed me his game and we played together. It was smooth sailing from there. Alfie understood I was his daddy's friend and he'd be seeing more of me, but I stayed away to start with when he was over at the house, so he had time to adapt. From there I slowly just built his trust up to know I wasn't going anywhere.

AMELIA, BLENDED FAMILY OF FIVE

TIPS ON MEETING TEEN STEPCHILDREN

DR DOMINIQUE THOMPSON

» Keep it low-key when you meet them. A simple 'Hi, nice to meet you' is fine. Be friendly and smile, but don't be over-the-top. Teens are very sensitive to emotions (their brains literally feel discomfort and moods more strongly), and they value their personal space. Respecting this will set you on a good path.

» It is a fine balancing act between being friendly and being distant with new stepchildren, and one you will become all too familiar with, but it is the route to success. Err on the side of being friendly but not over-friendly at all times.

» Building trust with teens is a 'long game', so try not to expect to make great strides in the early days. Be pleasant and interested and know that, with time, this will create a much stronger relationship.

» Be consistent. Successful families are built on stability. Your partner's teens will usually have had upset and disruption in their lives, so they need to know that you will be a constant, reliable, kind and safe option.

» Don't offer them gifts early on. You don't want to be seen to be trying to 'buy their affection'. Thoughtfulness and sensitivity in your behaviour towards them and their parent will be noticed and valued above gifts.

» Ignore any rudeness or sarcasm. It's not about you, it's about the position they find themselves powerless in, so they may try to take control of the situation by using drama and bad behaviour. Don't be drawn in. Rise above the poor behaviour, let it go and leave it to their bio parent to deal with it if necessary. Much of this will settle in time if ignored.

» Be a role model. Science has shown that stepchildren watch and evaluate stepparents' behaviour, judge it and then relate to them accordingly. If you are calm, respectful and kind, they will notice this, even if they still feel upset about the situation. Never shame them, as this is one of the most powerful negative emotions for teens and can cause lasting damage.

HOW TO PREPARE

There are lots of ways you can get ready for the challenges of your individual stepparenting situation, and we'll cover the more practical things in Chapter 3. For now, though, it might be worth considering the following:

Work and finances: How will blending families affect your job and career? You may need to work more to cover added expenses, or work less to devote extra time to the children. Think about whether your lifestyle expectations will need adjusting: holidays, trips, presents, treats. Will you need to have a stricter budget?

Your relationship with your partner: As we've already seen, you need good, easy channels of communication between you so that you can talk about your doubts and difficulties as you work out how to share family responsibilities. Be prepared for your discussions to last long into the night!

Friendships and family relationships: Are your family and friends on board with the changes in your life? If they're not, this will bring added pressure and stress. How do you deal with critics? Try not to listen to negative noise. How will your extended family look now? Will you have a relationship with your partner's ex and their family?

KEEP EVOLVING
SOPHIE RANTZAU

It's important for both partners to be honest about what being a parent/not being a parent looks like to them and to hear the other person's perspective as well. Keep talking because people's views can change: to start with, the biological parent might say that they're not expecting you to parent the children. Then there'll come a time when you move in, or you go out somewhere, and you ask, 'If they do this, can I say something?' It's time for another conversation.

For me, learning how to stepparent is a bit like learning to drive. We come fresh out of qualifying and we can almost hear our instructors saying, 'Mirror, signal, manoeuvre.' But before long, we get our own feel for driving – and we all have our own ways of driving, don't we?

BE KIND TO YOURSELF

There's no doubt that blending is difficult, especially at first. You're supposed to act like a family and get along with the children when you don't really know them. And if you're not very confident, you may feel as if everyone's ready to criticise when you make a mistake: 'Oh, that's exactly what I thought she was like!'

Remind yourself that it's not an easy situation and give it time. There are lots of mistakes made when you're in a blended family because you're in a position you've never been in before: you're navigating a new path, you don't really know everyone, you don't know exactly what you're doing. But you're trying your best, and your best is good enough.

Blending is going to open you up in all kinds of different ways! And, yes, in the course of all of this, you will feel vulnerable at times, like you're being judged and you have to prove yourself to everyone, which is something I'll be discussing later. For me, the first step to moving forward was acknowledging and owning my doubts and fears.

Parenting is hard and I am so hard on myself – I'm my worst critic. The things that have helped me along the way are:

» Acknowledging my feelings and, however small they are, accepting that's it's OK to feel like that.

» Sharing how I'm feeling with someone else – sometimes just saying things out loud makes everything feel more manageable.

» Getting some fresh air – clearing your head can work wonders in tough times.

» Reminding myself that my role as a stepparent doesn't define who I am. It's so important to remind yourself of the person you are and your qualities and strengths.

Tip: **I'm a big believer in manifestation – visualise yourself at your happiest. What changes need to be made for you to get there? I always said, 'I'll have a big family.' And here I am with three beautiful stepkids and now my own birth son, and I feel like that whole situation was just meant to be. There is a greater being or force that puts you where you're meant to be at that time. I'm a great believer in that.**

One of the Blended mantras is: 'A child's mental health is just as important as their physical health and deserves the same quality of support.' If your goal is to care for your step-children's overall well-being, focus on your own strengths and use them to be the best parent you can be.

CHAPTER 2

HANDLING CHILDREN'S BIG FEELINGS

'When little people are overwhelmed by big emotions, it's our job to share our calm, not to join their chaos.'

Children experience the break-up of their family as a loss. The old normal has gone, along with routines, traditions and time spent with both of their parents together.

The family situation may have been really difficult for everyone involved, but that doesn't mean that the children wanted it to end in separation – and even if the break-up seemed calm and well managed on the surface, it probably felt pretty disruptive for them.

Families breaking up often leads to other upheavals, from moving home to changing schools, so it's going to be a confusing time for kids, and possibly traumatic. As a result, the initial blending period won't be easy for anyone, but especially not for the children, who will have to adjust to living with a new family arrangement.

A child's sense of loss can feel a lot worse if one parent moves away, perhaps to live with another partner, or if they are absent because of mental health issues or addiction. All of these losses may be experienced like a bereavement by children, and they are likely to be grieving in one way or another when you meet them, even if it's not apparent.

In this chapter, we'll discuss the impact of both divorce and bereavement, as well as offering advice on how you can support your stepchildren when they are experiencing difficult feelings. We'll also delve into how to bring two sets of children together into a blended family.

HOW TO DEAL WITH CHALLENGING BEHAVIOUR

LAURA HERMAN

It's important to understand that underlying any frustration, anger and hostility your stepchild might be showing, there may be guilt about abandoning the parent who has been absented from the family or a sense of being disloyal. Even if they don't seem to care, they actually feel very guilty if they feel they've upset either of their parents.

My advice would be:

» Try not to have unrealistic expectations.

» Take it very, very slowly.

» Accept that this young person needs time.

» Don't push it – let the relationship evolve.

BLENDING AFTER DIVORCE

'Divorce isn't such a tragedy. A tragedy is staying in an unhappy marriage, teaching your children the wrong things about love. There is light after divorce.'

The most common backdrop to building a stepfamily is a break-up or divorce. Whether this break-up is friendly or fierce – or something in between – has a huge impact on the children. If the adults are largely happy with the way things have worked out, their children are likely to be more accepting, especially if the bonus people coming into their lives are fun and loving.

Some children are pleased when their parent starts a new relationship, especially if that parent has been single for a while and the child senses that they would be happier in a relationship. Others secretly – or not so secretly – wish their parents could get back together. Whatever they're thinking, your starting point as a stepparent will depend partly on what happened before your new family blended, and to what extent the children were aware of and involved in the changes that occurred.

> *I don't lie to my children, but they don't need to know everything. They don't know that their dad had an affair and I would never put them in that situation. Too many people don't think about the children enough; they are so consumed by their own pain and grief at the end of a relationship that the children part goes out the window.*

> *And actually I went the other way. However sad I am,*
> *I'll do everything I can to make sure things are stable for*
> *my children. I'll deal with my emotions separately, and*
> *never in front of the kids.*

SHANIA, BIO MUM OF THREE

Children will inevitably pick up on one parent being angry or unhappy after a break-up, and even though this can't be helped, they can be shown that their parent's resentment or sadness is not their fault or their responsibility, although it won't stop them worrying about them.

On top of this, there could be a number of other challenges:

» They may find the new living situation difficult. This can be a particular problem if they find themselves sharing a bedroom for the first time.

» They might be struggling with seeing their parents in a different light: one parent may be much happier, or stressed because of the changes that are happening, or sad because they're living without a partner.

» Their siblings might be behaving uncharacteristically. Maybe the eldest, usually the most confident, is now feeling shaky, or the normally docile youngest is acting up. Everything will feel wobbly and unfamiliar if siblings are stepping outside their usual roles.

» Perhaps their place in the order of siblings has changed. If they are blending with other children, the eldest child may be superseded and become a middle child, or the youngest might lose their place as 'the baby of the family', eroding their sense of identity.

» They may feel pressure from their other parent's family not to accept their new family set-up. Even if they don't express their disapproval outright, children are sensitive and pick up on unspoken feelings.

» Perhaps they're being teased at school about the changes that are happening, the fact they've moved into a different home or to a different area.

I had first-hand experience of this growing up. My parents divorced when I was around four years old and this had a huge effect on my childhood and teenage years. To put it lightly, I wasn't the most co-operative of kids!

I always hear people saying that children are resilient but, as parents, we're the ones making the decisions to make up/ break up. Imagine not being able to make those decisions and just having to go along with it. It's hard for children. When I was younger, I felt misunderstood and that my voice wasn't heard. I felt confused about what had gone on and, to this day, I still don't fully know what happened.

I feel like my childhood experience has really helped me in my role, on the other side of things, as a stepmum. Without realising it, my parents divorcing at a young age and me having a few different stepmums has helped me become the best stepparent I can be as I'm aware of how it feels to be a child coming into this.

For me, communicating, being open and taking on children's feelings and emotions is a huge part of being a stepparent. The most important things you can do at the start of your journey are to be open, listen, be there and show that you care.

STICK TO THE TRUTH –
AND KEEP IT SIMPLE
SOPHIE RANTZAU

If a child has parents who are splitting up and, say, one parent moves into the spare room, it's common for the child to be told that the move has happened because one parent has a cold or snores loudly, when actually it's because they're never going to come back to the marital bedroom. Fundamentally, that's a lie, which is not a great foundation for a child's understanding of the world, especially if they're very young.

You don't have to say much, or overload them with information. It's enough to say: 'Mummy and Daddy prefer sleeping in different bedrooms now.' It's important to be honest but also to explain a situation simply and in an age-appropriate way.

After we separated, my ex and I thought it would be good for our children if we did a lot of family stuff together still, like celebrate birthdays and go out on day trips together. So for one of their birthdays, we went to London for the day and to the theatre. It was lovely and everyone was happy until, halfway through the day, my son got upset.

When I asked him what was wrong, he said that he couldn't understand why his dad and I were fine and having fun with the family, but couldn't be together any more. It was then I realised that our plan for fun family days out wasn't going to work and the children needed

> *to know that the separation was real so that they could*
> *grieve and move on.*
>
> AINSLEY, DIVORCED MUM OF THREE

BLENDING AFTER BEREAVEMENT

'Grief is relentless, but so is hope.'

ZOE CLARK-COATES, BESTSELLING AUTHOR,
SPEAKER AND FOUNDER OF THE MARIPOSA TRUST

A grieving family is different from a standard blended family, and I've dedicated a whole section to bereavement because it was my starting point as a stepparent.

Forming a new family can be challenging as not all family members will be grieving in the same way, and some may not feel ready to accept a new situation. If your partner's bereaved children do not live with you, there may also be practical considerations such as: who will the children live with; will they have to move away from friends and family; will they need to start a new school? This can create extra difficulty and stress.

Whatever the situation, trying to form something new when everyone is holding onto what they had can be difficult. As a stepparent, the first thing is to recognise these losses and take things slowly.

I met my stepchildren, Lorenz, Tate and Tia, in 2017. Their mum Rebecca had passed away two years before and, shortly after I met them, their nan – who had become like a mum to them – also passed, so they went through a double tragedy.

I found it a real struggle coming in as a stepparent for children who had lost their bio mum. I tried my best to understand what they were going through but I never really will because I didn't know their mum and I don't have that loss. If I could bring Rebecca back, I would in an instant because of the pain that I've seen in them. A child losing their parent is just horrendous.

When you come into a family that's experiencing grief, it's an absolute whirlwind. My heart went out to the children; I desperately wanted to bring some happiness back to their lives. As a parent or stepparent, when you have a child, you just want to take all their pain away, but in this situation it's not possible. This is something I still struggle with. You just want to scoop them up and bring their mum back to make them happy, but you can't and it's tough. However, there are different ways you can support them in their grief.

I made it my job to find out more about childhood bereavement so that I could help my stepchildren in their grief and understand what they were going through, as best I could, and I'd like to share that with you now, in case it can help you in the same way.

What is grief?

Grief is a natural response to loss and encompasses different forms of emotional suffering, including confusion, sadness, frustration, anger and denial.

There are so many different levels of grief, and grieving is not a linear process: there's no timetable for how long it lasts; there's no set way for it to unfold. When a child is grieving, their emotions can get mixed up and lead to behavioural problems, or be suppressed and then pop up unexpectedly when they don't seem relevant or there's no obvious trigger. Children can also act out their pain or turn it inwards.

DEALING WITH ANGER OR REJECTION
DR EMMA SVANBERG

All children will experience feelings of anger, hostility, grief and upset around big changes happening in their lives and family. At times of transition, big feelings are not only to be expected but really to be welcomed. The more children can talk and show their feelings about big changes, the more they can move forward. It is when we add in other feelings like shame or repression of feelings that they tend to hang around for a long time.

All children will also go through periods of rejecting a parent – that might be you as a parent who they see as being the cause of a change or it may be you as a stepparent who they are finding hard to accept.

It can be unpleasant to face feelings of anger and rejection, but it can help to imagine yourself as a container. You're like a big jug that is able to be filled up with those difficult feelings, without judging them or taking them to heart. It can help to have a few things up your sleeve to help withstand the 'I hate yous' or the slamming doors: keep your own body calm, and know that you can be a strong and steady presence when the world is changing.

Children can express their feelings in ways that can feel deeply hurtful. It can help to see that as an expression of distress rather than, in the heat of the moment, get into teaching lessons about manners or politeness.

» Allow everyone lots and lots of time. If things have been said that need to be repaired, you can do that in calmer moments. But, like all relationships, this might take time to develop.

» It's helpful to deal with ruptures and repairs yourself rather than get a partner involved, which can create additional conflict and confusion. This will take practice!

» Make sure you also have a container – a friend, family member or therapist you can take all of *your* difficult feelings to.

Grief looks different for everyone

It's so difficult to support a grieving child because you just want to make it better. Grief affects people in different ways and children often experience aspects of anxiety, low mood, insecurity, anger, lack of self-esteem, trust issues, self-blame and difficulty sleeping or coping with change. These responses can be expressed at such a low level that they are barely notice-able; they can also be painfully obvious, even destructive. And it's not going to be one or the other – it can easily be a mix, depending on the child's temperament.

My stepchildren were all of different ages when their mum died and they all deal with it completely differently. The older boys have more memories of their mum and Tia struggles a bit with the fact that she hasn't. It's really hard because each of them is grieving differently and has different recollections.

In our case, I just try to support the kids in whatever way I can – whether that's sitting with them, listening to them, or just cuddling them and chatting with them when their feelings overwhelm them.

Finding love and 'moving on' when you are in the thick of grief might feel impossible. But, sometimes (and often unexpectedly) you're able to let new people into your lives and hearts. Rio and I and the children are a prime example of this. Love literally comes when you're least expecting it.

Think about the language you use

What I've learned along the way is that the language you use when speaking to bereaved children is really important – the way that I would talk to our two teenage boys compared to Tia is very different, for example. Sometimes I just don't know what to say, and I've made mistakes in the way I've phrased things.

I've learned over the years that you just can't pussyfoot around the word 'dead'. Something Steve Bland (who lost his wife Rachael to breast cancer) said on the *Blended* podcast really struck a chord with me: that the ways we have of couching death – 'Mummy/Daddy has gone to live in the stars' – are quite confusing for kids. They don't know whether they're going to come back or whether they've done something wrong to make them go away. As harsh as it sounds – and it took me a while to truly get on board with this – it has to be acknowledged that the person has died and isn't coming back. You've got to bite the bullet and be honest.

When they're ready to talk, they'll talk

At certain times, none of the kids might want to talk and I'm left feeling that I'm not doing enough. But I've also learned not to force them to talk about their mum or nan if they don't want to. It's a hard one to gauge, but I find it helps to just be there for them and to let them feel their feelings.

It's really important not to push and prod too much. Children can feel overwhelmed by strong emotions and may not always feel able to express them through talking. When they're coming to you really upset and can't explain it, doing a workbook together, making a memory jar (see page 89) or just going for a walk can help to alleviate the pressure, and give a child space to express what they think and feel.

I was very conscious of the fact that the man I had met had been completely and utterly in love with his wife, and she had died. 'Is it too soon for him to have another relationship?' I kept thinking. 'Is he ever going to love like he loved before?' I was feeling all these self-centred emotions. Then his five-year-old son came into the mix and, although I didn't ever shy away from the huge responsibility of bringing him up, I had all kinds of worries: 'What if I do it wrong? What if his mum's family don't agree with the things I do with him or say to him?' I started to question all of these things that as a parent you do very naturally.

I wasn't grieving anybody, but these two people that came into my life were, and I had to learn how to deal with that. Then, of course, as I became a part of their lives, I did start to grieve because I'd look at this little boy and my heart would break because his mum wasn't there. As much as I absolutely adore his dad and him, I have this huge guilt that I'm here and his mum's not. So it's a really bizarre process.

My six-year-old daughter is very inquisitive and wants to know everything, which is a lovely trait, but at the start I kept thinking, 'What if she asks the wrong question? What if it sets off an emotion?'

Luckily, my daughter and stepson just find this way to talk about all the stuff that you, as an adult, worry about and that they, as children, seem to take in their stride. He's very good at letting his emotion out. If he's feeling sad about his mummy, it will normally come out at bedtime and she's the first one to shout down the stairs to one of us, 'Come upstairs, quick, quick, quick! He's feeling sad.'

FAYE, BLENDED FAMILY OF FOUR

Grief can surprise you

As a stepparent coming into a bereaved home, you can sometimes find yourself in situations where you feel like you're walking in the steps of someone else's life. But what's strange is that I found myself grieving for Rebecca when I moved in with Rio and the children, even though I didn't know her. I remember thinking it was so weird at the time, but when I googled, 'Can you take on someone else's grief?' I realised that it's actually normal. Other stepmums and stepdads have said the same.

I remember feeling really guilty that I was upset because it wasn't about me – I didn't even know Rebecca. But then when I took some time and thought about it all logically, I came to understand that it's like there's a connection between us: both of us being mums to the kids, me knowing what it must have felt like as a mum to leave her children, as well as me wanting to do the right thing for the kids that Rebecca would be happy with.

What an odd feeling it is to feel sad and wish that your husband's previous wife would come back for the sake of the kids.

Things that come with the loss of a parent that you might not be expecting:

» Lots of comparison: this can be so detrimental to your mental health – comparison is the thief of joy. I always say that two people can exist side by side and be equally amazing.

» Big feelings around the deceased person. You may feel strangely attached and feel like you are building your own relationship with them.

» Resentment from extended family and friends of the deceased.

» Big emotions around special occasions. Make sure to be easy on yourself as well as your family. You may end up taking on everyone else's feelings and emotions.

More on all of this later in the book!

I've learned a lot about how to support grieving people, but I feel as if you can never really be prepared for grief. It helps to know that it comes at random times when you're least expecting it. Grief doesn't always hit you on the day you expect it to – it can catch you off guard. You can plan for Mother's Day, you can prepare for birthdays and Christmas, but you never know when grief will come, and it's always going to upset you when you see the children upset, whether or not you're their biological parent.

The blame game

We've seen that grief can affect people in different ways at different times; and, as the stepparent, you can often find that you're at the receiving end of other people's anger and frustration. It's widely accepted that anger is one of the stages that grieving people go through on their journey to accepting what has happened, but that doesn't make it easy when it's directed at you. In fact, it's far from easy.

One stepmum I spoke to – Faye – came up against resistance from the brother of her partner's late wife:

> *Nothing has ever been said to me, but the first time I met Amanda's brother, I could see quite clearly that he felt very uncomfortable. I don't think he could really deal with me – or not so much with me, but with the situation as a whole, and the fact that his sister's husband had met somebody else.*
>
> *I was very respectful of his feelings and didn't push. I will always be polite to people – I'm not going to be rude to anybody – and slowly but surely he's come around. I think there's probably been lots of talking with his mum and his wife, who have been a lot more accepting.*
>
> *I think it ultimately comes down to the people and their grief. You can let it eat you up – like bitterness, it can destroy you. But equally, you can look at it and say, well, this is not what I want, but I accept what it is.*
>
> FAYE, BLENDED FAMILY OF FOUR

It's a really difficult situation, isn't it? I feel for anyone who's going through it. It's hard enough being a stepparent;

the feeling that someone doesn't want you around is going to make it even harder to feel secure in your role.

There are two takeaways from Faye's story for me: the first is that she had the patience and compassion to give the brother time to process her arrival on the scene, the second is that he overcame his feelings by talking about them with other family members who could see the bigger picture. Eventually, he was able to put the happiness of his sister's husband and child before his own sadness and sense of loss, which must have made him feel a lot better, along with everyone else.

It's so worth fostering a more positive attitude towards the new family structure if it will help a bereaved child or children to live a happier life.

It's really important to me that we keep the children's life before me still very present, with their mum and everything that happened before me, and for the children to know where they come from. Rebecca is a huge part of our lives and is often in our conversations. I know so much about her now, so it's easy for me to bring her up with the kids and try to get involved where I can. Sometimes this works; sometimes it falls completely flat!

Me wanting to know so much about the kids' memories and their previous life, and the kids sharing it all with me so openly, is a testament to our relationship. However, it has its downsides too – if I'm feeling fragile and I have too much info about Rio and his previous wife, it can become very heavy for me. It is a real balancing act and this is why you really need to take time to sit and understand your emotions and how you're feeling, which is something we'll explore later in the book (see pages 146–8).

I don't want the kids to ever feel bad about anything with regards to their mum. If they're upset about something, they know they can come to me and I'll try to help. I'm not saying I *can* help, but I'll always try. I'm here to look after them as if they were my own children, but number one for me is to always emphasise that I'm not trying to take the role of their mum. The way I see it, Rebecca started the job and I'm finishing it. All three of us – Rio, Rebecca and me – are the kids' parents.

Tip: **When the comparison gets too much, try to remind yourself that you're doing a good job and you bring your own unique set of qualities to the family.**

It is difficult to understand what to do to help a stepchild who is grieving a parent, so I've included some advice here from Child Bereavement UK:

Children cope with the death of someone dear to them in their own individual way. Here are some things to consider:

» 'Clear, honest and age-appropriate information.'

» 'Reassurance that they are not to blame and that different feelings are OK.'

» 'Normal routines and a clear demonstration that important adults are there for them.'

» 'Time to talk about what has happened, ask questions and build memories.'

» 'Being listened to and given time to grieve in their own way.'

SHOWING SUPPORT

'A healthy stepmother knows that some days she's a stagehand, some days she's the leading lady and some days the audience ... and she plays each role with grace and style.'

Whether you're a biological parent or a stepparent, it can be hard at times to know what your children are feeling or thinking, especially when they've been through something as big as divorce or bereavement.

However, there are a few general tips below that I've drawn on over years to help support the kids.

Stepping back

As much as I want to make everything better and be the one to comfort the kids, sometimes I need to realise that I might not be the person they need at that particular time.

For me, it's about knowing when to step back – when to be there and when to not be there. I'd love to get involved and do everything, but every now and then I ask the kids, 'Do you just want to be with Dad? I'm happy to stay or go.'

I think it's about reading the room and knowing when I'm needed and when it might be better for me to make myself scarce. It's all a learning curve and, as with everything, it takes time.

Again, I find that the language you use here is really key and it's important not to make it seem like a big deal if I'm picking up on the feeling that I should ease myself out of the conversation. The kids know I'm always running around frantically, so I say that I'd absolutely love five minutes of peace – or to have a shower with no one running in! (I didn't even realise until I had kids that having a shower in peace just wouldn't be a thing any more!)

We cover imposter syndrome later on in the book (see page 176), but this kind of situation can really make it pop up. It's difficult to hear that all your family want and need is to have a discussion without you. Although it's hard to think like this and it can bring up strong feelings – I've sometimes wondered what on earth I'm doing here – it's about recognising those feelings, acknowledging them and knowing that it's quite normal to feel like this. Understand that by doing this you're doing the best for the child.

It's in these moments that you can feel very alone, like no one understands you, so I want to share my top tips here to stop yourself feeling left out:

» Call a friend.

» Read a chapter of your book.

» Do something you've wanted to do for a long time.

» Listen to a podcast … maybe try *Blended!*

» Go for a long walk.

It's so important to try to occupy yourself in these moments, otherwise your head will run round in circles. Trust me, I've been there!

Dealing with overwhelming feelings

When she was younger, Tia and I created code words to help us when she was feeling overwhelmed. Green and purple were her mum and nan's favourite colours and, if she was feeling upset, but we were somewhere she didn't want to say it out loud, she might text me or say, 'Green and purple,' and then we could go and have a chat.

Make a mind map

This is something we've used in our family and it really helps. A mind map is a way of creating a visual picture of thoughts and feelings using circles, arrows, single words or phrases and drawings. It simplifies complex ideas and helps to make sense of them.

1. Write down the problem or challenge in the middle of the page.

2. Draw lines coming from the problem and write or illustrate the different factors that have an impact on the central theme.

3. Talk (and doodle) as you go.

I drew the mind map on the next page as an example for you, and it's actually helped me feel better – this isn't just for kids!

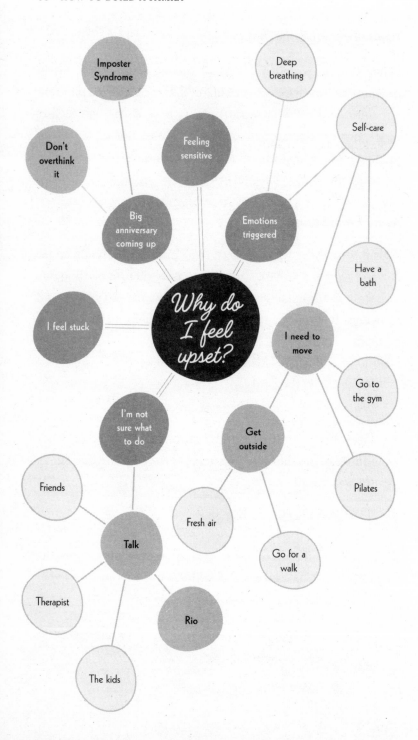

Another way to help children understand their emotions is by just sitting together and talking through how they're feeling:

'I really want to see Dad, but I feel worried.'

↳ 'Why are you worried?'

↳ 'Because I miss you all when I'm there and it doesn't feel like home, but I don't want to upset Dad.'

↳ 'What can we do to help? How about you take something cosy that feels like home, like your dressing gown and slippers? We could have a video call at bedtime so you can say goodnight to everyone and I'll speak to Dad about you feeling worried so he understands.'

However you approach this, it's about trying to get practical solutions to their concerns.

Try a worry monster

This can be a great way to encourage younger children to express what's on their mind. A worry monster is a cute(ish) fluffy toy with a zip up mouth and an inside pocket where a child can place a note that describes a particular concern they may have, for example, 'I missed Dad today' or 'What if Mum is late to pick me up from school?'

The idea is that if the note is popped into the monster's mouth before bed, the worry will be eaten up by morning! It's up to parents or carers to empty the pocket while the child is asleep – and subtly address the worry at a later point.

Write it down

For some children, sometimes just writing things down – in a note, a letter or journal – is a great way to keep dialogue and communication open about ongoing feelings and thoughts. Kids don't necessarily want to talk when you do or they might feel uncomfortable discussing certain topics – instead, they can write down their thoughts and leave it out for you to read and acknowledge. Equally, you can ask a tricky question and

To Kate,
I am not writing this to get my phone back I just want to apologise for everything. I know it was wrong to go on my phone when I shouldn't and to be honest I don't know why I did it.

☆Night
Night
love u
loads

To
Kate
And
Da

encourage your child to write a response when they are ready to give one, or simply enquire about the best/worst things that have happened that day to give them a framework for what to write in a daily journal.

This may seem simple, but I've found it really helpful.

Things often feel big and overwhelming until you put them into perspective. I've found it helpful to rate some of those things on a scale of one to ten. If it's below a five, we know it's not that much of a big worry. If it's above a five, we can sit down and try to figure it out together.

Chat when they're distracted

Sometimes it's easier to introduce difficult subjects when the children are doing something that already partly occupies their mind. (Although not when they're on their screens as they won't even hear you!) You could have a chat with a younger child while they're playing with Lego, or you're washing up and they're drawing at the kitchen table; you can talk to a teen when you're in the car and they don't feel the pressure to make eye contact.

Coping with change

A child expressing unhappiness about the way things have changed could simply be them trying to process what has happened out loud, so try not to ignore or brush their misgivings under the carpet, and don't feel offended. Instead, acknowledge their feelings and maybe even ask a few questions, before moving on to focus on a more positive viewpoint.

Remind them of the things that haven't changed: maybe they still visit their gran on a Sunday, go to a weekend club, sleep with a favourite toy or get sweets on a Friday as usual.

They can still have their friends round. In the meantime, set up and stick to new routines and introduce the idea of new rituals and traditions to integrate into the family framework (see page 87 for more on this).

Communication, communication, communication

Whatever you're going through can make you more emotional in everyday life and that's why it's really important to communicate. We all might have a different opinion on something and not agree, but at least we know how everyone feels.

In our house, everybody has a voice – and I think it's really important that the children know that. Good communication is at the heart of positive family relationships.

Here are a few tips for communicating with the children in your household:

» Put your phone away before you talk. Ask them to turn off technology too. Getting rid of distractions makes talking special. This seems simple but can be hard in this day and age. It's worth it, though – you'll both be able to focus and you will avoid temper flares when one of you gets distracted and drifts off …

» Where possible, try to have some one-to-one conversations. Don't rush this time, and try not to check your watch or phone while you're with them. Wait for a natural break in conversation before you say it's time to go.

» Listen and show you're listening. Encourage your stepchildren with comments like, 'That's interesting, I'd never thought of it like that before,' or 'I can see you've really thought about this.' Empathise before you put forward another point of view – say, 'That sounds difficult,' or 'How did that make you feel?' Look at it from their point of view first, even if something doesn't sound right and you want to point it out.

» Timing is key. There's no point in starting these conversations when you're all rushing out the door to school or work. Try to find a time when you're all relaxed to talk to the children about their feelings or behaviour.

I'm not saying that there won't be times when things get heated and emotions run high, but I've found that just keeping the lines of communication open is the first step to calmer family life.

It's also worth bearing in mind that parents don't always know what children are dealing with on a day-to-day basis. Sometimes we might think they seem sad or quiet because we're divorcing, or because a new stepparent has come into the family, or a step-sibling is in the next room, when actually it's not that at all and we're overlaying it with our own interpretation.

BLENDING CHILDREN

Bringing two sets of children together can be one of the hardest parts of blending, especially if the differences between them are very marked. They may differ in age, talent, learning ability and appearance; they may have been brought up with different values and expectations. Some of them may be used to having their bio parent to themselves; others may still be adjusting to a more recent separation between their parents.

When my partner and I decided to introduce our kids to each other, we looked into books and other resources to help with blending families and started reading a lot. My partner is from California and, in America, it is common to see family therapists to ensure you are doing all the right things in preparation.

The therapist we saw helped us think about how we were going to introduce our five children to each other, any situations we wanted to avoid and how they might take to us and to each other.

It was also useful to understand that, while we were crazy about each other, that didn't necessarily mean the kids would feel the same about the whole situation. The books we read also helped enormously. There were things we hadn't considered, such as the natural and then imposed birth order of the children. So my son, who was used to being the eldest, would then become the middle child – quite a change!

With hindsight, some of the things we did/read/prepared for were great and much needed, while others didn't end up being relevant. For instance, we were advised to be cautious and not to spend too much time all together to begin with, as the children might not want to. But, to our surprise, and very happily, all five of them absolutely loved meeting each other and demanded regular time together, including sleepovers. So some of the advice went out of the window because we were responding to what the kids wanted.

CHLOE, MUM OF TWO, STEPMUM OF THREE

Sibling rivalry can cause friction within any family, but it can get really complex in the blended world. The obvious scenario is of two sets of kids vying for status in the new family structure, but it could also be that older siblings feel jealous when a new baby is born. In this scenario, children in a blended family have an added layer of envy to contend with – because, while their parents have split up, the baby's parents are together. This sometimes leads the stepparent (the baby's bio parent) to bend over backwards not to show favouritism and to make sure their stepchildren feel just as loved.

That's definitely true in my case – I worry about the big kids so much more than my biological son, Cree. Sometimes I feel that the love you have for a stepchild can be even more intense because you've worked so hard to get there, and I find myself overdoing everything. Maybe that's partly because there's a different kind of worry that comes with children who have lost a parent, but it probably applies to a lot of stepparents. If you're aware of past trauma or sadness in your children, you're always going to try to help them through it.

When I compare myself with some of the mums I know, I see that I'm much harder on myself when it comes to Lorenz, Tate and Tia. I'm always questioning myself and second-guessing things – what would their mum do? Am I doing the right thing? With Cree, I just don't question myself in the same way.

DEALING WITH FAVOURITISM

DR EMMA SVANBERG

One of the hardest things about experiencing favouritism is the guilt that we feel as a parent. But all parents might favour one child over another, whether they are biologically ours or not.

Favouritism tends to come from finding one child easy, and often that stems from how complementary our personalities are, the interests we share and the time we have spent together. This happens in all families – as in all relationships, we fit together more easily with some people than others.

However, clear favouritism can impact on everyone involved, causing conflict between partners and siblings, as well as affecting a child's sense of themselves within the family unit.

Rather than trying to treat all children the same, it can help to accept that there are going to be differences between them. They are different people with different needs. So, instead of asking, 'How can I stop favouring one child?' we could ask, 'What can I offer these children according to their different needs and different relationships with me?'

It was pretty tough at the beginning blending two older boys with two younger girls who were all used to their hierarchy in their original sibling order. The oldest boy and the oldest girl struggled the most. I don't know if it's a first child thing, but each is quieter and more sensitive than their sibling.

When we met, my partner had a dog, which really won over my girls, and four years ago I also got a dog. Two dogs definitely adds to the chaos, but helps bond everyone too. Five years on, the boys have great relationships with my girls, when they aren't fighting. They are all into music and drama, so our nickname is 'the dysfunctional Von Trapps' and we couldn't be happier!

ZOE AND KATH, BLENDED FAMILY OF SIX (PLUS TWO DOGS)

Dealing with conflict between siblings

Like the rest of us, children are individuals and can be wildly different from one another. They can get on, or not; they may have shared values and perspectives, or nothing in common at all. The fallout of conflict between the kids in your family can be massive – and there you are, the stepparent, stuck in the middle of it all, trying to create harmony. Whether you get involved or duck and let the bullets fly over your head is something to be discussed with your partner.

Sibling tensions can affect you directly in several ways: you'll feel torn if there is conflict between your biological children and your stepkids; if one or more of your stepkids tries to persuade the others to have a negative view of you; if one child refuses to co-operate with you; or if they call you out as a stepparent in public, to make you feel separate to the family.

TIPS ON DEALING WITH SIBLING CONFLICT
DR DOMINIQUE THOMPSON

» Never compare siblings or step-siblings. Everyone is a unique individual and creating conflict or resentment will be detrimental to any relationship-building in the family as a whole. Instead, try to comment on positive attributes, keeping it low-key or gentle, not over the top. Let them know you have noticed a good idea or effort with a smile and a 'Nice one'. It will go down well whether or not they acknowledge it.

» Include everyone in decisions and plans so that no sibling feels excluded or forgotten.

» If step-siblings are peers in age, this will add a level of anxiety as they will be supersensitive to what their peers think in general (the teen brain is driven to focus on peers more than family in the adolescent years). It will be like having the volume turned up on any comparisons or criticisms, and being sensitive to this will help smooth things longer term.

» Be aware about being fair in your behaviour otherwise the children will note and possibly resent anything they see as being unjust. This can be about the size of their rooms, the amount of space within that room, time spent helping on homework or whose friends come over more. Be tuned into 'fairness' and you will avoid some of the potential arguments!

» Stay neutral when it comes to sibling arguments. Do listen patiently to outpourings of confusion and

> angst, and be sympathetic, offering kind and wise words, but avoid any disparaging comments and never criticise the other child.

It's really important to me that all four of my children – step and biological – are treated the same and feel equally included in the family set-up. I pride myself on that. But because there's such an age gap, I was concerned about how the kids would bond. I was worried that, when Cree was born, he would feel left out. The other three kids have shared a loss, which gives them something to bond over – something in common – and I was concerned that it would be three and one rather than four. I also worry about how I'm going to explain to Cree that I'm not the others' biological mum when he's a bit older – I worry about the grief pouring into him as well.

It's still early days, but it's so special to see the way the other kids are with Cree – they have really embraced him into the family and he has brought us even closer together.

My stepdaughter has two older brothers and one of them didn't see eye-to-eye with me for a few years, although we have an amazing relationship now. He would remind his sister continuously that I wasn't her mum. She found this difficult, especially as her mum didn't give her as much attention as I did – I was the one helping her with homework and listening when she was upset. Eventually, in her confusion, she went to live with her mum for a while, to try and nurture more of a mother–daughter relationship. But it didn't work and now she's back with her dad and me and we have a great relationship again.

SOPHIE RANTZAU

I hope these ideas will help you, but keep in mind that support can look like lots of things – a quick text, a little note in their lunchbox or a hug. It doesn't always have to be deep.

As a stepparent, you can help children to cope with change and loss by creating a home that meets their practical needs and offers safety, stability and warmth, which we'll cover in the next chapter.

CHAPTER 3

BUILDING A FAMILY

'Family is family, whether it's the one you start out with, the one you end up with or the family you gain along the way.'

There are no hard and fast rules for making a blended family work because everybody's situation is different. It's not like starting a first family, when you follow pregnancy guidelines and look out for set baby milestones; there isn't a rule book and there's no gradual easing-in process. You don't get a chance to test the water; it's more like a dive-bomb and whoosh, you're in another life.

It can all feel a bit overwhelming, so in this chapter we'll look at all sorts of practical things, like what the kids should call you and that big step of moving in together, as well as offering tips and advice on making memories as a new blended family.

But first, it might be helpful to be mindful of a few things as you start out …

You can't build a family overnight

It takes time to adjust to living in a blended family. Often you can feel like you're failing. I first met Professor Lisa Doodson when

Rio and I were filming our documentary. I was really struggling at the time and she had so many answers for me. Something I remember her saying is that it takes between four and seven years as part of a stepfamily to feel relaxed and for everybody to settle into their new roles. I thought at the time, 'Shit, I've still got at least another two years!' It really freaked me out and I was left wondering, 'Am I going to be able to do this? Is it going to get better?' In my case, it's taken five years to fully find my feet as a stepparent. I now feel much more settled in the home; we all understand each other and know how everyone works.

The first year or two is definitely the hardest because there's so much happening – you're getting to know each other, building relationships, establishing new routines and adapting to daily life together. It's a lot! For some families, it takes longer to get settled because of changing circumstances: shifting custody arrangements, the family expands, previous partners get married, parents' jobs and finances ebb and flow. Life constantly evolves and changes as families grow, so go easy on yourself – these things take time.

It might sound like a way off before you reach that point where everything is calm again, but have a little hope that it will be OK and, as time goes by, you will start to feel more comfortable in your role.

Love grows

Love can be instant, but it usually takes time, especially if people are feeling hurt and pain from what's come before. You will probably need to build up trust and respect first of all – and then love will hopefully follow, for all of you.

Give yourself and everyone else the time and space to become familiar with each other.

Your relationship will need to adapt

In the early years of blending your families, unless you knew each other before you got together, you and your partner are still getting to know each other and building a loving relationship. This is happening within the very specific context of at least one of you having children from a previous relationship, so you can't necessarily expect things to follow normal patterns.

Romance, passion, excitement and laughter can still be the beating heart of your relationship, but more thought and planning may be needed to make space for them. And, let's face it, sometimes you're just going to be way too tired for any of it!

It's fine to wing it sometimes

It takes time to build confidence in your role – I'm sure I'm not the only one who'd admit that I was winging it for a huge chunk of the early years (I still am now), hoping that no one would notice how uncertain I felt. I went into this family feeling confident that I could handle pretty much anything, so it came as a shock every time I came across a situation that I hadn't foreseen or couldn't fix – like when the doctor asked me if the kids had had their jabs (more on that later!) or when the kids ask me about memories of their mum and I just don't know the answer.

These days I'm more accepting of the fact that half the time I'm improvising. I've also had to work to let go of my tendency towards perfectionism, so that now I feel a lot happier about going with the flow.

WHAT SHOULD THE KIDS CALL YOU?

Finding your feet and knowing what 'terms' to use can be tricky in the beginning. This was really confusing for our kids in the early days and it took a while to figure out what they're comfortable with. For me, it's about going with the flow and, whatever the kids are happy with, I'll follow suit.

To be honest with you, I don't love the phrase 'stepmum', but it's what I am! We've thought about other phrases, but none of them feel quite right. Over the last five years, at times I've been called 'Mum' by my stepkids, but now we've settled with simply 'Kate'. I know a lot of people use the term 'bonus', which might work for you.

> *I've started calling my stepchildren my bonus children. I've noticed that it feels different when I don't say stepdaughter or stepson.*
>
> SOPHIE RANTZAU

When Cree was born, I was really worried about how the other kids would feel when he started calling me 'Mummy'. Our house has always been safe and I was concerned it would bring up feelings for them hearing me being called Mummy. But, actually, as with many things, it's all now fallen into place. I'm now 'Kate' *and* 'Mummy' in our house.

I had a moment in the lead up to one Christmas where I got myself in a real pickle over personalised stockings and PJs. I know it may sound silly, but it really played on my mind!

I love being 'Mummy', but I didn't want to just slot myself in as Mummy where Rebecca was before. (I really do over-think everything!) Something just didn't feel right about being

Mummy when all our names are in a line together on the mantelpiece, so I went for 'Mummy Kate' – and it worked.

Until you're in a situation like this, it may seem very silly to worry about seemingly little things like this, but it's just another one of those awkward things that sit differently for blended families. Another example is when the kids write their dad a card: he is simply 'Dad' or 'Daddy'. Being 'Mummy Kate' in situations like this means that all four of my children can write the same card for me as one. It's so important to me that all my children are as one and that Cree isn't separate.

As the family has evolved, so has the terminology we use … it's about being flexible. We've had this discussion as a family and it's something we're all happy with. You've got to do what feels right for you as a family and not get hung up on 'labels'.

It has worked for us to feel our way when it comes to what the children should call me, but if you strongly feel one way or the other, it's definitely worth having that conversation early on to avoid confusion.

IT'S ALL A LEARNING CURVE

When you come into a family, there's so much to learn about the children: what level of practical help they need, what emotional support they require and how they show their feelings. If you haven't been a mum before, or if you haven't been around kids of their age, it's quite hard to find it all out at once.

In the early days, I was so overwhelmed with everything I had to remember – the obvious things like dinner, bath time and the school run – that the smaller (actually quite big) things, like cutting toenails, totally slipped my mind.

Blending families can also mean blending cultures and things crop up as you go along. My children are mixed race and, when he was younger, Tate had beautiful curls that you can only dream of, but they weren't so beautiful after I'd brushed his hair! It makes us laugh now, but I have memories of him screaming while I was brushing out the tangled knots – I just didn't have a bloody clue. You really are learning on the job. Tate has cut his hair off now – but I promise it's not because I couldn't manage it!

We put so much emphasis on getting things right and pressure on ourselves to be perfect, but that's just not reality – you can't get everything right. Things will go wrong and I think that's fine.

MOVING IN ... BRACE YOURSELF!

Honestly, I underestimated how difficult moving into the family home would be. In some ways it's easier if you already have children, because you'll understand that looking after kids is hard work as well as fun and rewarding. But if you start off your stepparenting journey on your own, as I did, it's more difficult to prepare for what's in store.

Moving in with Rio and the kids is one of the hardest things I've ever had to do. There's so much that comes with moving into an already-made home. It just wasn't my house, and I missed my home comforts and that feeling of safety. One minute you're free and independent, the next you're adapting to somebody else's schedule and getting your head around the logistics of the school run, after-school clubs, bedtime routines and what everyone likes to eat for dinner.

Not only did I now have children to care for on a daily basis, I didn't know where anything was and I was surrounded by lots of possessions and memories from a former life. I was well out of my depth. To put it frankly, it just wasn't my home and it's taken a long time for me to feel relaxed here.

My flat in Essex was quite modest, but it was the perfect cosy home for me. Now I'd moved into a house I could have only dreamed of as a child, and yet I found myself longing to be in my flat every day.

A big worry for me when I first moved in was what my role was and how I would fit in, and I think it's something a lot of people struggle with. Added to that, I had all sorts of other worries, like:

> » Am I going to be compared with their mum all the time?

> » Am I getting things wrong?

> » What do I do when one of the kids wakes up in the middle of the night?

> » Can I discipline them? How do I discipline them?

> » What would their mum do?

The positive thing about moving in with your partner is that it means you're in a good place in your relationship and you're ready to take it to the next step. You've overcome so much together already where a lot of people would have given up.

It's still early days, though, and moving in is a big step, especially when blending families, so in this section, I want to discuss the common hurdles people face and hopefully give you some ideas and tips to make the whole transition that little bit easier.

Start with the practical things

Just a word of warning: this isn't going to look like how you see moving in in the movies! This is the blending of two households and it can feel really overwhelming. There is so much to think about, even down to the little things, like what to do with all the furniture.

I found it helpful to start with the practical side. If you've got some stuff under control and running smoothly, it can help to make things feel less overwhelming. Here are some of the things you might want to think about:

The home:

» Who's going to sleep where?

» What about food? What do the kids like to eat?

» Whose furniture are you keeping?

» How many mugs does a family actually need?!

» Where do the pictures go?

» What are we going to do with all the *stuff*?!

We adapted our dining room into another bedroom and made sure that we had a bit of space for all the kids to call their own (well, three girls in one room!). We're doing OK so far!

LAURA, BLENDED FAMILY OF TEN

Work:

> » How will blending two families affect your work schedules?

School:

> » How are the kids getting to school?
>
> » Who's going where after school?
>
> » Are there after-school clubs to consider?
>
> » When do they need their PE kits?
>
> » Have the children's school been told that you will be doing pick up?

Other:

> » Is the car big enough for everyone?
>
> » If you're with the kids and you're in a medical emergency, who is the next of kin?

We were still driving two separate cars when we first blended, as we couldn't fit all the children into one car safely. We did this for a few months and then sold both of our cars and bought a seven-seater. This made our life easier, especially for my husband, who could get on the train to work in London while I did the school run on my own, in one car. It was also better financially rather than paying for two sets of petrol, finance and insurance.

NICOLE, BLENDED FAMILY OF SEVEN

There's a lot to consider, but go easy on yourself. It is a challenge to move into an environment where you don't know the children fully and everyone has a different way of doing things. As the saying goes, you never really know someone properly until you live with them. It really takes time to get to know each other's routines, habits … and irritating traits!

Give yourself time

This is a transitional time and it will take a while to find what's right for your family unit. Moving home is stressful enough as it is, let alone with a whole new family set-up to consider.

I moved in with Rio and the kids gradually: in the beginning, I would come over for a few hours and go home, or I would do a school run one day. Just bits and bobs like that. I was around quite a lot, often to organise doing something fun, but then I'd go home.

I met Rio about six months before his mum died and I was by his side at the hospital during that very stressful time. This was when I first started staying over a few nights at the house with the children and I began to know my way around; then we went on a couple of holidays together. There came a point when Rio and I realised that, for the kids' sakes, we either had to do this properly and put everything into it, or it wasn't going to work. We decided to go for it and in the autumn, I moved in.

We involved the children every step of the way and Rio made them a big part of the process. They gave me a moving-in gift of a blanket covered in photos of us all and a pair of slippers for the house – how lovely is that?

I was born and brought up in Dubai and originally come from an Asian/Arab background. I met my husband through work and, when I met his four-year-old son, I instantly loved him like my own and wanted to give up everything to be a stepmum to him. I can't imagine loving anyone as much as I love him.

When my husband proposed, I quit my job and constantly travelled to the UK to spend time with him and his son, whose mum lives in Wales. My husband is an offshore engineer and is often away; I was travelling between Dubai and Wales. But my stepson needed more stability, so I decided to move to mid-Wales permanently to help his mum look after him while my husband was working on a rotational basis. I wanted to be there for my stepson 100 per cent. I wanted to see him grow up, to love him, care for him, take him to school, take him for tuition and take him to football. My husband and I moved to where his school was, not far from his mum.

I was completely out of my comfort zone in mid-Wales. Coming from a bustling city like Dubai, I found everything and everyone a little difficult. I felt I had no place. All my family and friends were in Dubai or in London. I found solace in the knowledge that I had moved here to create a wonderful life for my stepson. I put my stepson first and I would do it all over again, but I couldn't have done it without my husband's support.

A couple of years on, and I'm a full-time stepmum to my stepson. We share him with his mum but we spend a lot of time with each other, especially when my husband is back from work. My stepson tells everyone he has two mums and loves me as his third parent. My heart swells with pride when he hugs me or tells me he loves me.

MAHVISH, BLENDED FAMILY OF THREE

Making a house a home

Cosy is a feeling as much as a look – it's as much about having a sense of being warm and safe as it is about zipping up your onesie and snuggling in front of the telly. Warmth isn't just about temperature – it can also mean affection, friendliness, comfort and hospitality. And safety is about much more than having solid walls and doors with locks that loudly click.

How do you make the best, cosiest version of your home, so that you and the children feel welcome, safe and happy within your four walls? Below are some tips that might help:

» Think about what is important to each of you that you really want to keep. What makes you feel at home?

» Get new photos taken of you as a family. You can all pick which photos you like and put them up around the home.

» Smell is a big reminder of home, whether that is candles or hand soap, so try to have some familiar brands and scents scattered about the place.

» Try to take away the expectation that every room is going to feel homey. Maybe make one room – say, your bedroom – your own so you have one small space where you feel comfortable and you have somewhere you can run away to if you need to just take a breath. If you can feel comfortable in one room, that is a good start.

» Try to keep the kids involved – it's about their little add-ons as well. Rio and I went out with the kids and chose some lovely soft, cosy blankets together so the kids had a say too.

Making changes

When I first moved in with Rio and the kids, I just slotted into their way of life – I felt as though we needed to continue their way of doing things. But this gave me some identity issues and it soon became clear that we also needed to make some memories together and adapt to the new family set-up.

I know I'm not the only stepparent to find that there are difficult conversations to be had about things changing in the home. It can be hard to bring things up initially, but once those conversations are had and everyone has been given a voice, including the children, as a family you can feel better about the change and move on.

You can't do these things quickly, though. It's not about changing things straightaway. At the forefront of all of our decisions was (and still is) how this would make the kids feel and this then guided us through each decision we made.

Tip: Before we made any big changes, Rio and I made little alterations like buying a new bed and some new rugs. I also changed the soap in the bathroom to my favourite scent and brought my big fluffy blanket with me from my flat. Those little things really helped and made me feel like I had my home comforts.

After two years and lots of conversations back and forth with Rio and the kids, we felt it was time to make some decorative changes to the house and take the next step as a family unit.

The kitchen is the hub of our home and so we decided to start there. It's a big change that could have meant upheaval for the kids if we didn't do it in the right way, so we tried to get them involved as much as possible: the paint samples were dabbed on the walls and the floor options were all laid out, and the children would come and say which they thought would be best. We all love the new kitchen now and it really feels like our special place.

Making decisions as a family

We try to involve our children in a lot of our decisions. Sometimes that means giving them options that we've already approved, but at least they then feel they have a voice and are involved. Don't get me wrong, we still make a lot of decisions for them. For instance, if they say they want to go to bed late, I'll say, 'No, you're going to bed now.'

But in other situations, we involve everyone in the conversation. 'We're thinking about getting a takeaway. What do you guys think?' We'd then have a vote – who

> wants Chinese, who wants Indian, who wants pizza ...
> (Mind you, if the vote doesn't go my way, I'll still order
> what I want ... lol!)

We also had to make a decision about what to do with the photos of Rebecca that were scattered around the house. It's hard when life is moving forwards to make the person who has passed away still present and I feel like you need to really work hard at that because those memories can slip away. It's such a fine balance making sure you feel comfortable in your own home while not erasing the other parent's memory, but we came up with creating a room we now call 'Mum and Nan's room'. It wasn't easy making this change and, again, we had lots of conversations, but the children chose their favourite pictures of their mum and nan and we reframed them and put them up in this room.

Making changes like this is about give and take, about the children feeling that they have a voice and about all of you coming to some sort of agreement together. We still sit in Mum and Nan's room, and we still talk about both of them. Now we're all comfortable and we're all happy because there's space for everyone.

It sounds easy when you say it like that, but it wasn't! It took a while. For me, it wasn't about removing Rebecca's presence from the house; it was more about creating a happy space in memory to the kids' mum and nan. It's important to me that we keep their memories alive.

I also like to think that, if it were me who had passed away, I would still want my photos around, but not so that it overwhelmed the kids. All of the children also have photos of Rebecca in their bedroom, which means they have a few places they can go when they want to see their mum.

For me, home should be a place full of fun and love where we all feel comfortable to be ourselves. You can't be the best version of yourself if you don't feel relaxed and comfortable at home. Children, as well as adults, should feel free to express themselves and be who they are; home is where they have a voice and their opinions are listened to and heard. We all have a contribution to make; we all need to feel happy and safe.

It's tough when you come into an already-formed family and you're trying to find your space and change the way certain things have been done and still respect what has happened before. As you've seen, it took a while for us to get there and I never thought I'd feel at home as I walked through the front door, but I feel that now. Our home belongs to all of us.

> *I remember the negative thoughts I had in the years after I moved into my husband's family home with my child from a previous marriage. I started off thinking, 'Is it OK to change a picture?' and it got to a point when I thought, 'Is it ever going to be my home?' I made changes very slowly and very carefully; it was never about getting rid of his wife from the house; it was about finding my place in our home.*
>
> *I still get upset and feel guilty for asking to move a picture, even though my partner says, 'Yeah, of course, just do it.'*
>
> *I have to say to myself, 'But it's my home now, as well. I'm here bringing up these two children in the home that, yes, my partner and his wife shared together before she died, but now we share together and she's very much part of it.' But feeling that I belong here has taken a long time and*

> *I still have those doubts. I still have moments now where I think, 'Am I living in somebody else's life or is it my life?' and I have to tell myself, 'No, it's your life and it's a good life and you're surrounded by lovely people and you have incredible children that love you.'*
>
> *And that's all that matters really, isn't it? As long as they're happy and you're happy, then whatever noise is going on outside it is exactly that – it's noise that you can't control.*

FAYE, BLENDED FAMILY OF FOUR

MAKING MEMORIES

Although I haven't experienced a lot of the children's 'firsts', because I wasn't there, we have made many special memories together that will last a lifetime. I have to accept that I didn't experience their first steps or their first word, but I can be happy that I experienced Lorenz getting his braces, Tate's first day in Year Seven or the first time Tia did a certain jump on her horse.

How to boost your memory bank

» Try something new together; do something for the first time.

» Celebrate individual triumphs together. ('Do you remember when we went out for an ice cream sundae after your dance competition?')

» Set achievable shared goals (serious or silly) and celebrate when you reach them.

» Take lots of photos so you can look back and reminisce together.

» Start new family traditions, like having a takeaway every other Wednesday or a fry-up on a Saturday morning, going for a walk on a Sunday morning, making each other cards/choosing flowers or certain foods for birthdays, or unwrapping one present each on Christmas Eve.

Make a photo album

I'm a fan of making photo albums that we can sit and look through when we've got a few minutes to spare. The kids and I love to look at how small they were when I first met them, compared to how they are now, or giggle at funny photos of Ronnie.

I've made a photo book of our first moments together. There's 'The day Daddy and I met'; 'Our first date'; 'The day Ronnie and I met Lorenz, Tate and Tia'; 'My first sleepover with you'; 'Our first holiday together' and lots more. All the important memories of my first year with Rio and the kids are there and we love looking back at them. Photos take you right back to the moment and jog memories that you'd forgotten. They also remind us of how far we've come. There's one picture that really stands out for me – we are all splashing and dunking each other in the pool on that first holiday. We were having so much fun and I remember thinking, 'I can't believe it! This is the family I've always wanted.'

It can a bit time-consuming to make an album – honestly, I'm a year behind on mine! It's on my very long to-do list, but it keeps getting put to the bottom – but, when you can manage it, it's well worth it.

Revisiting memories and key times in your family's past becomes more and more meaningful as the years go by. I love the idea of one day showing my albums to my grandchildren! But in the meantime, they bring us all a lot of pleasure to remind ourselves of the road we've been travelling and all the highlights and funny moments along the way.

Design a photo calendar

I know that some families like to choose the best or funniest photos to put on a wall calendar that you flip every month. It's a simple pleasure, but kids love it. You could theme the photos to match the seasons or have a shot of the kids diving off rocks on holiday as your January image – to perk everyone up at the idea of the coming summer, start you all reminiscing, and as a reminder to book your next holiday!

Make a memory jar

The children have done this since their mum and nan passed away – they write memories and put them in a jar or box and are free to pick them out and read them whenever they want to. This works really well and might be a nice idea to try for your new blended family.

When you become a stepparent, all you can do is try your best. Know that there will be mistakes along the way – I've made mistakes, the family has made mistakes – and you don't really know what you're doing. Looking back in hindsight, I can see all this really clearly now, but when you're in that moment, it's tough.

You have to be pretty resilient and adapt and change to fit into an already-formed family unit. It isn't always easy, but it's often filled with a new love that you just can't explain. Trust that there is light at the end of the tunnel: love is such a powerful thing.

CHAPTER 4

BONDING

'Being a stepparent means they grew inside of my heart instead of my tummy.'

Your new family is taking shape and finding its own rhythm, but when are you actually going to feel like you all belong together? In our house, we are one: me, Rio and the children. But it hasn't always felt that way and it has taken time and patience to get here.

In this chapter, I'll be sharing my thoughts about how to strengthen the family unit and giving you an idea of some of the potential pitfalls along the way. We'll also look at how we can all make the best of coming together as a family in terms of our behaviour. As ever with stepfamilies, there's no simple answer, although, as we've seen, patience, love, empathy and adaptability will get you a long way in creating positive patterns for happy blending. Oh, and I'll be reminding you to have fun (again!) because fun is one of the core foundations when you're building a family.

FEELING LIKE AN OUTSIDER

Sometimes, no matter how hard we try to feel a part of our partner's and children's lives, we can feel like an outsider at times. I still have up and down days, but in the beginning, I found it really difficult because I felt as though I was coming into this already-made family with this already-made life and I was kind of on the outskirts. I didn't really know what was going on. And because of everything Rio and the kids had been through, everyone would always ask me if they were OK, but they never thought that the person stepping in might be struggling as well. It's hard, but this is why I like talking about it. Until you go through it, you can't really understand – people don't get it.

It's not nice to feel left out, but it's something I still struggle with and, to be honest, I think I always will. It has no bearing on how Rio and the children treat me; it's much more to do with entering an already-formed family.

No one means to make me feel excluded, but it's inevitable because there are years of family life that I wasn't around for. So, we'll do something fun and it'll be my first time, and Rio and the children will say, 'Do you remember when we did this before?' So many memories had already been made before I became a part of their new chapter.

As much as I love to learn all about their life before me and get involved as much as I can, the fact of it is I wasn't there. And it can be the tiniest thing that can get me in my feelings; I am highly sensitive and have always craved love, a big family and to feel safe. I often can't believe my luck that I have the things I have always dreamed of, but weirdly, at times I feel like they're not really mine.

Navigating your way through this and trying to find your place can be extremely difficult. It does become easier with time, but do these emotions ever fully go? I'm not sure. Will I always feel not fully part of everything? Maybe.

There are so many examples I could give you that made me feel uncomfortable in those early days, but there's one that has really stuck with me.

As you walk into our home, there's a spiralling staircase and, when I first moved in, behind it was a huge wall full of photos. Arranged as a family tree, it cascaded down from Rio's and Rebecca's grandparents all the way to the children. You could see this beautiful family from the minute you walked in as well as every time you went up and down the stairs – and from room to room – which meant it would have been such a huge change for the children if it was taken down. But it also meant that I couldn't escape it without just having tunnel vision and walking everywhere with my head down. It was awkward. It felt like I was walking through someone else's life – that I shouldn't really be there – and I was embarrassed to invite my friends over.

Despite all of this, I still feel that keeping the photos up was the right thing to do for the kids at the time. Rio was hyper aware that he was bringing someone else into the family home and he instinctively knew that not everything could change at once. I think he made the best decision as a parent and I'll always respect him for those tough decisions he had to make in the early days.

Even looking back I feel emotional as it brings back all those feelings of vulnerability. I didn't feel 'safe' in my home and I also felt I was being judged by the whole world. I think it's fair to say that it's taken a lot of healing and self-care to get where we are today. As with so many aspects of building a stepfamily, these things take time.

And just in case you're wondering, a huge mirror is now in place of the family tree. It was important to us that we didn't replace Rebecca's photos with mine and that's a respect that runs through everything we still do today. I'll never be a replacement for Rebecca – I like to see myself as a third parent.

> *'Blood makes you related;*
> *love makes you family.'*

It's inevitable that if a family was a family unit before you, at certain times you're going to feel outside of that. For me, this already-formed family is really my whole life, yet they had a life without and before me. It's a hard thing to get your head around at times.

The reason we can feel like an outsider is because, biologically speaking, we are. But love goes beyond blood and I do believe that love conquers all. To my fellow stepparents, this is an amazing but difficult and confusing journey. It can be bloody hard work. If you feel like an outsider at times, please know you are not alone. All we can do is try to cling to the positive and not dwell on the moments of doubt.

TAKE IT SLOWLY

It sometimes feels as if I became a stepparent overnight, but actually it was a process that went through several different stages. It's important to be clear that, when you move into an already-made family, the children aren't necessarily going to love you instantly, or even like having you around. Firstly, they've got to get used to you and get to know and trust you.

For us, that process happened quite quickly, partly because I'm a full-time stepmum and also because my children were missing a mother figure. But I can imagine things going a lot more slowly if you're a part-time stepparent and the other bio parent is very actively involved in the children's lives. I know this can be hard, but, remember, good things come to those who wait!

> My wife's children (11, 12 and 14) can be quite mean to me. The youngest, a girl, isn't so bad, but the two eldest boys are challenging to be around. They keep talking about memories from before I knew their mum; they never stop saying that their dad is good at football and computer games and a million other things.
>
> My partner doesn't seem to notice and that's hurtful too. When I brought up how I felt about her children being hostile, I talked about it more as a challenge they were experiencing. I didn't blame them or criticise them directly, so she didn't feel she had to take sides. But after that, she made a point of turning conversations around to bring me in, and when the boys said their dad was good at this or that, she talked about what I was good at and I felt reassured, even if it didn't change much to start with. We're good now, the boys and me. I take them fishing and their dad doesn't fish.
>
> SIMON, BLENDED FAMILY OF FIVE

When I first met Lorenz, Tate and Tia, their dad and I used a few tricks to ease things along. In the beginning, I'd turn up at the house for a 'date' and we'd pop around the corner for a quick drink – not for so long that they would notice particularly or worry that I was taking Rio away.

When we came back, I'd spend time doing fun things with the kids, so they knew that every time their dad went on a date with me, they'd have loads of fun afterwards. They linked the two together and started to like seeing me – and then when they were asleep later, we'd go out properly. They were younger then and we'd never get away with going out later now that they're teenagers; they would know if their dad went out at nine o'clock at night. But the principle is the same, whatever their age: if something good happens for them when their parent's new partner appears, they are more likely to accept – and even welcome – the new partner's presence.

PRIORITISE THE KIDS

I believe that the key to building a happy stepfamily is making the children your priority wherever possible. This may involve putting your own feelings aside at times as you help the children feel safe and secure in the new family setting. It's a lot of work, but the rewards are amazing.

If you make the children your priority when you become a bonus parent, one of the first things you have to take on board is that your relationship with your partner will often take a back seat. There may be times when that's hard to accept, but in the long run it makes sense for both you and the children, because if they're not OK, you and your partner are never going to be happy.

I've always tried to make sure the foundations with the children are really strong. I feel so lucky to have a good bond with all of them now. They taught me how to love a child before Cree came along.

CHILDREN COME FIRST

LAURA HERMAN

As a new stepparent, you may want to focus on your partner, but in an ideal world, if you want to really invest in this new family and make it work, the children have to come first. Because if the children are causing conflict, there's going to be conflict between the parents.

IT'S THE LITTLE THINGS THAT COUNT

'Trust is not built in big, sweeping moments. It's built in tiny moments every day.'

BRENÉ BROWN, AMERICAN PROFESSOR,
LECTURER, AUTHOR AND PODCAST HOST

In order to bond with your stepchildren, you need to relate to one another in a meaningful way. Obviously, this depends a lot on the children's ages, but I think my main piece of advice to really connect with the kids would be to find out what they are interested in and research it. Then you've immediately got something to talk about! You will be halfway there because you can speak to each other – trust me, it really helps to start building that bond.

When I was getting to know Lorenz, Tate and Tia, I found out which rappers and musicians the boys liked and talked to them about music. I now also know all about football, so I can get involved in those conversations too. I actually surprise them with how much I know now, and I *kind of* know what I'm talking about – lol!

You can really bond with children over the little things – anything that shows you care and that you're interested in the topics they like. When I was first getting to know Tia, she enjoyed horse riding and feeding carrots to the horses – she still does – and when I came over, I'd bring along carrots and mints so that we could feed the horses together. Sometimes it's the really tiny things that can connect you: the kids had never had the kind of popcorn that you heat up in the microwave and I brought some along on our first holiday together. We'd sit in bed in the evenings loving our bowls of popcorn – and then every time I came round after that, I'd bring popcorn. I regularly did little things like that to show that I was consistent, and, as we'll see below, I think this is really important.

Relationships are dynamic and children are growing and developing, so nothing stays the same, but if you carry on helping them and showing an interest in their lives, I reckon you'll be OK.

KNOWLEDGE IS KEY
LAURA HERMAN

Accept your lack of knowledge and educate yourself. So, for instance, if you are moving into a stepfamily with teens and you want to have a good relationship with your stepchildren, then it might be worth learning a bit more about teens, if you've never had one, by reading books or listening to TED Talks – the cognitive neuroscientist Sarah-Jayne Blakemore has done some great TED Talks if you want to find out more about how the adolescent brain works.

We've talked about how it's the little things that start to build up trust and respect. The flip side of this is avoiding big, sweeping gestures that may overwhelm the children, especially if they don't know you well and haven't got a handle on your personality.

You're much more likely to build respect and trust with kids through small, thoughtful gestures, by displaying an interest in them and just showing up.

Tip: **I'm all for acknowledging the little things. I like it when people say I've done a good job, so I try to do the same with my kids. Although I still moan about silly things like leaving dirty pants and socks on the floor, I'm the first one to praise them when they've done something great.**

The most important thing about being blended is not how to be a perfect family, because they simply don't exist, no matter what Instagram or Facebook looks like. If you show up for all the tears, plasters on knees, bedtime stories, 5,000 toys in the bath, cuddles, holding hands to make them feel safe; if you show up when they are happy, lift them up when they feel frustrated or sad, listen to them, help them learn about the big world they are a part of; if you can bring joy, love and care to the little people in our lives, that is what makes a parent.

HANNAH, STEPMUM OF ONE

BE CONSISTENT

It took quite a while for the children to trust and bond with me. When I moved into the family home, I was there consistently and did the same things for them each day, like cooking dinner for them every night and putting them to bed. That structure and predictability made all the difference. After a while, the kids got used to me being there and started to enjoy having me around. If you're not consistent with kids, they don't know where they're at.

Routine is important in creating rhythm and structure in any household, but it's especially important in a blended home. Kids generally like to know where they are and where they stand – even more so after loss or trauma, when their world has been turned upside down. They find comfort and stability in knowing what's going to happen next, so try to plan and structure your days as much as possible. Morning and bedtime rituals, mealtimes and bath times provide a backbone to family life. Timings don't have to be absolutely fixed or rigid, but children like to know what's happening next and will appreciate being told in advance if the routine is going to change or be interrupted.

When I first moved in, the children were very anxious and it was clear they needed things to be predictable. If I said we were leaving the house at 11am and we didn't leave until 11.15am, they would start to get upset and one child in particular would cry. It was a problem because getting three kids out of the house doesn't always go exactly to plan – someone has always lost a shoe, or can't find something they want to bring with them. It can be difficult staying calm in those ten minutes when we're getting ready to leave, but the secret is to do everything with lots of time to spare, lol. Never easy, but I'm learning!

ALI, STEPMUM OF THREE

HOW TO KEEP A ROUTINE WHEN CO-PARENTING OVER DIFFERENT HOUSEHOLDS
LOUISE ALLEN

To co-parent successfully, all the adults involved need to behave like adults. Do you all genuinely have the children at the front and centre of your thinking? If your relationship is not great, then perhaps expect a few bumps in the road while you all work to create a safe adult co-parenting atmosphere for your children. If you feel that your routines are deliberately being hampered by the other parent/household, let it wash over you and do not let them know that you are bothered by their behaviour. Usually things settle down and life moves on.

Forgiveness and kindness are also so important. Sometimes the other co-parent may be late or experience issues that take their time and attention elsewhere. Be the better person(s) and support them. Perhaps offer flexibility into your routines that can work for all the households. Sometimes 'life' just happens and people are late or fail to meet a commitment.

» Think about the language you use and how you frame your messages. If items are regularly left behind at the other home, try not to get cross with your child or moan about the adults. That only instils negativity, which is damaging to your children. Just check in before your child comes home and ask if the items can be remembered.

» Routines do not have to be rigid; sometimes a respectful, relaxed approach is better for everyone. Create a fluid flow through all the homes that allows your children to feel that they are not satellites but embedded in all the settings. The routines will change as the children become older and you will have to move with your children's milestones.

» Decide what your new family culture looks like and arrange different activities that enrich all your lives.

» Do not compare yourself or your situation to others. Our children grow up remembering the quality of our love and commitment, not the money in our accounts, despite what they say when they're young.

» Create a culture of openness within your family and lead by example. If it's beginning to feel like you are the main parent for whatever reason, try not to feel resentful because those feelings will be passed on to the children.

» Plan your arrangements in good time for your co-parents to be able to co-ordinate their diaries.

Bedtime routine

Bedtime is a great time for kids and parents to bond. In the early years, I'd sit with each of the children for five or ten minutes in their bedroom while they went to bed; we'd have a chat and a cuddle and I'd stroke their hair or back. I've got to be honest, this felt like a real chore sometimes! It wouldn't happen every night and sometimes there'd be tantrums, but it's often in these moments that kids will tell you what's on their mind, or open up about the highs and lows of their school day. I know how frustrating this can be – you've got your evening planned, and you just want to jump in the shower and have a glass of wine – but this is a good time to help them resolve minor worries, or just have a giggle that will send them to sleep with a smile on their face.

Now they're a bit older, I'd absolutely love to get into bed with them and stroke their hair – especially the older kids – but they couldn't think of anything worse! (Isn't it funny how the things we once found a chore we then come to long for?) Instead, they now come to our room every night. I sit on the bed, they sit in a couple of chairs and we have a debrief. I love that! It's one of my favourite times of the day. They think they're too cool for me to come and sit on their bed at night, but we still have that time, just in a different way.

SPEND FAMILY TIME TOGETHER

We all lead really busy lives – in our house, we're juggling family life with work, football, horse riding … the list goes on, so sometimes it's difficult to get us all in the same place at once. But family time is SO important and, for me, it's when I recharge. I'm at my happiest when all my family are in one room.

Getting together as a family doesn't always have to be a big event – sometimes it can just be when we're all sitting on the sofa catching up or having dinner together after football practice.

In fact, most of our family chats take place when we're sitting round the dinner table on a Sunday. Eating together as a family is a huge thing for us. Where possible, we all try to put down our phones and have a good old catch-up round the table. It doesn't happen every day – the kids have so many after-school activities – but when it does it's a chance for everyone to have a voice. I'm sure sometimes the kids just carry on talking so they don't have to do the washing up though – I'm not sure if they're even enjoying the chat or not!

Getting everyone involved in cooking and preparing for a meal, even if it's just laying the table, also makes it a team effort.

Getting the kids involved in family meals

» Plan menus together. Take turns to choose dishes.

» Cook and prepare food with the children. Divide up tasks: one does a starter, one does the pudding, or shut them all out of the kitchen and tell them it's a surprise!

» Draw up a table-laying rota.

» For special meals, let the kids choose which tablecloth/candles/plates to use.

It can be hard to prioritise family time when juggling three extended families – mine, Rio's and Rebecca's – and everyone wants to see us. Throw into the mix friends and work colleagues and things can get really hectic. I found this hard at the beginning, but now I make the six of us having our own family time a priority.

Family outings

Often the main hurdle to going out for an adventure is getting the kids off their screens – you may have to lure them with the promise of an ice cream or a hot chocolate while you're out. You don't have to splash loads of cash to have a great day out, though. The main thing is that you go together and it's a shared experience. If we give the kids the opportunity, they'd probably prefer a lie-in – especially the teenagers – but once we're all out, everyone enjoys it.

One of our favourite things to do as a family (once we've got everyone out of the house) is to go for a family walk. We started to really enjoy doing this together over the various lockdowns during the Covid-19 pandemic, and now a mix of the fresh air, chatting and exercise gets us all feeling good. Find what's right for your family – it might be a trip to the local park, tennis courts or mini golf, a visit to the seaside, the cinema or a shopping centre, or even going to a museum.

Tip: **We tend to think that it's the expensive things that kids will love, but often it's the simpler things that everyone enjoys.**

TRY NOT TO COMPARE

I am the queen of comparison and, though it's natural to compare yourself and feel like you're not in the same place as other people, no one's journey is the same.

For the first few years of being a stepmum, I was guilty of comparing myself to all the 'perfect' families on social media, but now I realise we all just share our best moments, and I try to step away from social media and focus on the good times and the things we've got going on that are going well when things get tough. That's one of the reasons I set up Blended so that people have a safe space online to open up and be honest. Every blended family has a slightly different story but you can relate to different parts.

Another trap that stepparents sometimes fall into is to compare themselves with the previous partner. It's worth pushing away the urge to self-evaluate in this way, if you possibly can, because it's usually the situation that's at the root of any tension rather than anyone in particular. You're not the one deliberately making things difficult – and others may not be, either. No one is better or worse than anyone else – everybody is different, and people's differences need to be respected.

Here are some tips from the Blended community that might help:

» Accept that the children may insist very vocally that their other parent is fantastic. Try not to hear what they're saying as meaning *better*. They may be speaking out of a sense of loyalty, or to reassure themselves, to test you, rattle you or persuade your partner to get back together with them. Try to be compassionate, even if it seems like they're doing it to upset you, because they're probably not emotionally developed enough to understand what it means to you.

» Understand that you're not perfect. You are human, like everybody else. Nobody is a perfect parent, no matter how amazing they appear. The things the parenting manuals say you shouldn't do – like losing your patience or raising your voice – *everybody* does them, including the previous partner. We all make mistakes; forgive the children theirs and try to learn from yours.

» Be present for the children, listen to them; be as tender and patient as you can be with them. They will sometimes respond gratefully to your consideration and care, and in those moments you will feel fantastic. Hang on to those moments!

» Recognise that children are constantly evolving and it's sometimes challenging to keep up with the changes. Do they need attention or do they need independence? It's even harder to know this when you haven't raised them from birth, as their biological parents have. Sometimes you'll just have to ask them.

» Don't stress about giving the kids loads of stuff. Their bio parent may be materially better off, but as long as you've provided for their basic needs – and that includes a sense of safety and security – the greatest gifts you can give are your focused attention, your emotional support and your consideration of what's best for them. These gifts will in turn make them feel worthy of love and boost their self-esteem.

Remember, no family has the same path; all are beautifully unique. Be sure not to get lost on yours by comparing your journey to another's.

DON'T EXPECT TOO MUCH!

When it feels like everything isn't going to plan, it's hard not to feel impatient, but try to go with the flow and not put too much pressure on yourself. Nothing is going to happen overnight.

With children comes chaos – it's a fact of life – and so you should always expect the unexpected, or at least be prepared for it.

ONE SIZE DOESN'T FIT ALL
SOPHIE RANTZAU

Children are all different. For instance, my youngest stepchild wanted me to be mum, but my middle stepchild continuously reminded her that I wasn't her mum. We didn't see eye to eye – he fought me tooth and nail – and now we get on amazingly and he says I'm the best stepmum in the world. That's another reason you've got to be flexible. Nothing is set in stone.

It's a bit like Goldilocks and the three bears: you just have to see which bowl of porridge each child likes, or which story is good for them. They're not all going to be the same because we're not all the same.

TRY NOT TO TAKE THINGS PERSONALLY

Children can be direct and brutal. Their remarks can cut you to the core and make you doubt yourself. I am really guilty of this and automatically feel like people's words or actions are an attack on me personally.

I spoke to Professor Lisa Doodson about this and this is what she had to say:

HOW TO DEAL WITH HURTFUL WORDS
PROFESSOR LISA DOODSON

We're all human and, even as adults, we do get hurt by what children say to us. Children can push buttons, and sometimes they're pushing those buttons because they feel hurt, frightened or even angry. They have very little control over the changes in their life, so sometimes their behaviour is simply a reflection of this and a way of venting their frustration. They can have lots of different emotions that sometimes they can't express easily, so try to think about what's happening in the moment. Step back and understand why they might be behaving the way they are and whether there's something you can do to make things easier for them – and you! Make sure, though, that they know, if they're old enough, they have hurt you so it doesn't become a pattern of behaviour.

Everybody needs to understand that, no matter why you're disagreeing or how complex the web of feelings being triggered, it's not OK for anybody to be rude or aggressive towards anybody else. (Make sure you don't reaffirm this principle by yelling it! It's not a good look to shout at your kids for shouting, although we've all done it, lol.)

My advice would be to try not to react, but, in all honesty, I react way too often. Try to be consistent in your approach and keep a sense of humour where you can. None of this is easy!

REMEMBER TO BE SILLY AND HAVE FUN

Sometimes the stress of the house takes over and I am guilty of being a complete stress head. Every so often things just have to give – the other night we were all dancing round the kitchen being silly and letting off steam. It's in those moments when I feel really grateful and happy.

In my experience, children want attention, so as long as you make time for them, they start to enjoy having you around. Especially in our situation, where the kids had lost their mum, they enjoyed that motherly love and the fun that we had. They also liked it when I took the mick out of their dad with them and was 'on their side' rather than his.

Having fun with the kids helped me to establish a bond that led to trust and acceptance. It's a slow process, but you can take small positive steps every time you meet. Once I had their trust, I could move into being more of a parent figure to them and they could follow my lead. In time, they began to come to me for advice and reassurance.

BONDING AT DIFFERENT AGES

Bonding with a child of five is going to be very different from bonding with a teen.

HOW TO BOND AT DIFFERENT STAGES OF DEVELOPMENT
LOUISE ALLEN

Children under ten

» Let the children come to you; do not overwhelm them.

» Take an interest in them and learn about their world.

» Go slowly.

» You do not need to shower them with gifts that will be hard to sustain.

Tweens and early teens

» Let them know that you think they're important. Despite their occasional awkwardness and attitude, they still need adult attention and plenty of reassurance.

» Involve them in your plans and spend time on their interests.

» This age group like to spend time in their rooms, but still need to know that you are there when they need you.

Mid- to late teens

» Treat them as adults and respect their lives and choices unless they are unsafe.

» Try not to make them feel like you are the cuckoo in their nest. Give them space to adapt to the new relationships.

» Most importantly, be the version of family that works for all of you, recognise everyone's roles and laugh, a lot!

TIPS ON CONNECTING WITH YOUR STEPCHILDREN

DR DOMINIQUE THOMPSON

» Be patient. You are building a friendship, which takes time, and with patience and perseverance, acceptance of you as part of the family is absolutely possible.

» Be open. Avoid secrecy and secretive behaviours as this makes children nervous and unsettled. They will worry that they are being left out and won't understand why but will assume the worst. For example, if you're going out with your partner, tell the kids what you are doing, where you are going and when you'll be back.

» Give them space, both literal and personal – and respect it. If they are going to be moving between different homes, it is vital that they have a room they can call their own, even if it is shared with a sibling. If you are buying or renting somewhere new, include them in the discussions and viewings, and make sure they know they will have a room to sleep in and retreat to.

» Be a trusted adult in their life, but don't go behind their parents' backs. It's a delicate balance, but encourage them to talk to their parents too. Some topics you might be able to help with specifically, such as those related to your gender (periods or shaving, for example), and here it might be appropriate to be discreet, but never secretive.

NURTURE YOUR RELATIONSHIP WITH YOUR PARTNER

You and your partner won't always be in sync – because of busy work schedules and hectic lives – but as long as you keep communicating and try your best to support one another, you can get through the tough times.

Kids are territorial and possessive of their parents, but they also want them to be happy so that they don't have to worry about them. If they sense a parent is unhappy, it's going to be harder to have a good time themselves; they may be blocked by feelings of guilt and anxiety. So nurture your relationship with your partner, even if you don't have much time together – because the two of you are at the heart of your blended family; you are the very reason it exists. Your happiness won't guarantee absolute harmony among everybody in your household, but it'll make it a lot more likely that you'll all come together as one.

Having fun is a great way to reconnect. Rio and I are always saying we should plan date nights, but we don't do it often enough and probably need to make more of an effort. For us, though, it's often enough just to go for a walk. We'll have a chat, take in some fresh air and come back to the house feeling renewed. When you think of having time together, you always think it needs to be a night out or dinner – something away from the home – but you can keep it simple and just do smaller things to connect. Don't get me wrong, a date night is amazing, but it just can't happen every night. Try these other ideas to create moments of connection with your partner:

» Get up a little earlier and have breakfast together.

» Pick up the kids from school together and have a chat on the way.

» Have a movie night at home.

» Do a workout together.

> *Having one night away together doesn't sound like much –*
> *and it's not enough – but it changed everything to be away*
> *from the house and the kids, to put each other first for*
> *once and remind ourselves that we are people in our own*
> *right. We had such a great time that we're going to try to*
> *have a weekend away at least twice a year from now on.*
> *It was really bonding for us, as well as being a much-*
> *needed mental rest from the kids.*
>
> DANIEL, BLENDED FAMILY OF SIX

When I leave the kids for a night out or a few nights away, I always feel guilty, so I try to organise really fun things and for them to see favourite people while we're gone. If I know they're having a good time, I don't worry so much and can enjoy myself more. And when I get back, they haven't even missed me!

Communication

Love, commitment and trust come first, but how you communicate your love is also important.

Rio and I knew from the beginning that, if we were going to bond the family, we needed to think as a team, as well as a couple. To be a good team, you need to know you're on the same page as your partner, and staying on the same page means having conversations.

If something is bothering me, being open about my feelings makes me feel better. I can't keep things in; I like to get my feelings out there so that I can put that issue behind me and move forward. Sometimes I think, 'Maybe I didn't need to say that,' but at least everyone knows where I'm at! There are ways to say things, though …

» Say what you mean and say it with love, if you possibly can!

» Fight the problem, not each other.

» Don't bottle up resentments; deal with them now or as soon as you are able to broach your feelings in a calm space. Be honest and open, without being insensitive. Explain your feelings as clearly as you can.

» Listen to what the other person has to say. Don't interrupt. Be open to their point of view. (They may be right, after all!)

» Try not to sound accusing, by saying, for example, 'You upset me when you said …' You're more likely to be able to make a connection with your own emotional triggers if you reframe it as 'I felt upset when you said …' or 'It seems to me, but maybe I'm wrong …' This will help you decide whether whatever is upsetting you is your stuff or not. Also avoid saying, 'You should …' and 'You shouldn't …' as no one likes to be told what to do.

» Don't bring up old grudges; try to focus on the present and the issue at hand.

KEEP WORKING ON YOUR PARTNERSHIP
PROFESSOR LISA DOODSON

What's really important is not how the children behave or react with you, it's how your partner does. It's the couple that makes the blended family – without it, you're just two people in a relationship and you can quickly become two separate groups, each parenting their own children, which will only drive a wedge between you both. Of course you have to prioritise the children's needs, but if you don't put time aside for you and your partner, you can end up with disparate parts of a family. Make sure you spend quality time together, without the children, making memories and building resilience.

Never forget that you are here because of your partner and the love you share together. Always keep in mind how strong that love is and that everything springs from your relationship with your partner.

The wonders of gratitude

This might sound a bit cringe, but I am so grateful for Rio. I've always dreamed about having someone love me the way he does, and I know he feels grateful for me because of everything I've done for him and the family. We've been through so much in such a short space of time and we're just grateful we have the love and support of each other to get through.

Studies have shown that when you feel grateful towards your partner, you also feel more committed to them and prepared to work harder on staying happy and together. There is even evidence to suggest that being thankful is more important than being romantic in a couple relationship.

I've found that when I feel appreciated and loved, it allows me to be the best version of me.

Five simple ways to bring gratitude into your relationship

1. Focus on the positives.

2. Thank your partner when they do something nice for you and show you appreciate them for being the person they are.

3. Be generous with compliments and demonstrate your love – don't keep it to yourself.

4. Accept that everyone has annoying habits, including you! Let go of little niggles and remind yourself of the bigger picture.

5. Don't forget the importance of everyday touch and hugs.

'When love comes back into your life, when you find someone who is willing to give their love and their time and their efforts to your child, that's a remarkable gift, so always be thankful.'

SIMON THOMAS, FORMER SKY SPORTS PRESENTER

Getting married

Marriage is something I've always wanted – I've always dreamed about getting married – and it's something that Rio and I would talk about together and as a family.

Rio proposed on 31 October 2018 – I'm not sure if he was implying I'm a witch! The kids were there and we all went out to dinner that evening to celebrate.

Before we were married, I'd sometimes find it difficult because every time anyone referred to Rio's 'wife' they were talking about Rebecca, which made me feel like a spare part. After the wedding, I felt more secure and confident in my role as a stepmum. Rio would probably argue that I was secure anyway, but for me, personally, I'm really happy that we're married. It makes me feel safe. From the inside, we always were secure and stable, but other people might not have thought that. The wedding may have cemented that for other people.

Marriage can be confusing for children, though, so making them a part of the journey and your decisions is really important. Rio and I exchanged rings, but I also bought each of the kids a love bracelet to signify that it wasn't just about me and Daddy – it was about us all coming together as one.

It's important to bring the kids along with you every step of the way, from the early days of thinking about getting married to the day itself. We wanted the children to be a big part of our special day, so the boys walked me down the aisle and Tia was my maid of honour. All three of the kids gave speeches and everyone in the room was in tears. It was so special and we'll all remember it forever.

It can be incredibly bonding for the family unit if everyone in the new family structure gets on board and gets involved with a marriage, but for your stepchildren it may not feel so simple to see you and their biological parent making it permanent. They may have been secretly hoping there was still a chance their parents would get back together, even if all the signs are against it and in their hearts they know it's never going to happen.

HOW TO INVOLVE YOUR STEPCHILD IN A WEDDING

LAURA HERMAN

It could be a good idea to include your child and get them involved in the wedding plans, but I think it's important to ask them if they'd like to. And ask them what role they'd like to have, because I think that sometimes, in the desire to make them feel involved and make them feel special, they can be given something to do that they don't want to do. They don't necessarily want to be part of celebrating this new relationship, so always ask, always listen and don't make assumptions about what they're feeling.

Up until the point of Gary and I getting engaged and married, I think there could potentially have been the seed of a thought in some of the children's minds, especially Gary's children, that perhaps their parents would somehow magically get back together. I don't think this would ever have seemed like a realistic idea, as things were not very friendly; however, I do think some children have that idealistic thought process.

> *The gorgeous way Gary proposed to me – we were on safari in South Africa and he and his children proposed to me and my children – really started a huge excitement within our family of seven and our shared experiences and connection. They were so excited about the proposal; they were fully involved. They were bridesmaids and best men at the wedding and they were a huge part of the ceremony, followed by a familymoon for all of us.*
>
> *It was a beautiful episode in among what was a still rather challenging situation. But there was no denying that, at the heart of it, they were all extremely happy we were getting married.*
>
> CHLOE, MUM OF TWO, STEPMUM OF THREE

Our wedding day was the most amazing day ever – the best of my life. The wedding knitted us all together. Having said that, everyone feels differently about marriage and it's not a necessity to building a strong family unit.

Having a baby together

My biological son Cree is such a blessing and the icing on the cake to our blended family. He brings so much joy to our family and we're all so grateful for him. But when I was pregnant, my hormones were all over the place and I felt highly emotional about all sorts of things. I was anxious about how his arrival would affect the family. I also felt like Rio had experienced this before – three times over – but it was all new to me. It seems silly now, but I had feelings that I wouldn't know what I was doing and he knew everything and I worried whether he'd feel the same as me because it was my first child.

It's a unique experience having your first bio child but already having three children. I already knew how to parent from the age of six plus, but having a newborn baby was a whole other ball game. My friends talk about those early days with their first child when they were in a haze of feeding, sleeping and nappy-changing. I was doing all that, but also worrying about PE kits and after-school clubs. I just didn't have that first child experience.

All the kids wanted to be a huge part of being with Cree – feeding and helping to bath him – but, at the time, my hormones were all over the shop and I felt like I wasn't getting enough quality time with him. I had an emergency C-section and so having had major surgery and not being able to do the things I normally would made me a lot more emotional about everything. Now, looking back, I'm so grateful that they wanted to be so involved. I really feel like having Cree has gelled us together.

The impact of a baby

The arrival of a baby is always good news and it's generally a welcome development for the blended family because suddenly everybody is related to the new baby. Couples in blended families often see a new baby as a bridge that links everybody: the stepmum is mum to a baby who is the children's new sibling. If they are a stepmum's first child, it may bring her closer to her stepchildren in loads of different ways.

However, looking after a baby is a lot of work, taking attention away from the other children, and this could cause all kinds of conflicting emotions. The children may fear that the baby will be loved more by their parents. There could be jealousy around the fact that the new baby's parents are still together and sibling rivalry can bubble up and be played out through jostling for time/closeness with the new baby/child.

Tips to include the children:

» I bought Tia a 'big sister' book to help her understand what it was going to be like with a new baby in the house and how important her role is. She also bought Cree's outfit for when he came home from the hospital.

» All the kids helped us choose the name.

» I had Cree in lockdown, so couldn't have any visitors, but it's really nice if the other kids can visit the new baby while you're still in hospital.

» The kids could help you decorate the nursery or choose a small gift for the baby.

» You could buy a gift from the baby to the other children – this works especially well if they're younger.

Getting a pet

A pet can bring the whole family together – it can be really bonding taking them out for a walk, playing with them, feeding them and teaching them new tricks.

I came to the family with my dog, Ronnie, and we all love him so much – he's so spoilt. He's the king of the house!

Building a relationship with your stepchildren is going to be a gradual process, whether you live with them full- or part-time. The glue that will eventually hold you together is love (hopefully), but first come respect and affection, and each takes time to grow – for everyone.

And try to be grateful. As quite a few stepparents have said to me, one way or another, despite the challenges of becoming a stepparent, it is the most rewarding, wonderful gift that just keeps giving.

CHAPTER 5

DISCIPLINE AND SETTING BOUNDARIES

'The hardest thing about being a blended family is knowing when to fight and when to let it go.'

Discipline is hard in those early days as you want to be loved and accepted. It's like this fight inside you – you know certain things are right, but if you keep saying no, you worry that the kids are going to think you're miserable! But, in the long run, putting in those boundaries cements your new life and your new family set-up. In this chapter, we'll explore different approaches to discipline, as well as how to stay on the same page as your partner and the importance of boundaries.

I've read advice saying that children feel more secure in the first couple of years of blending families if they mainly look to their biological parent for love, care, behavioural expectations and discipline. That makes sense in some situations, but another option is for the biological parent to make it plain that they support the stepparent's decisions. Again, it's important that you're clear about your role and place in the family.

As a stepparent living full-time with my stepchildren, I needed to start as I meant to go on, once I'd moved in. It's inevitable coming from two different homes that you'll all have different ways of doing things, but I'm not here to be half a parent; I'm here to be a full parent – I'm fully a stepparent and so, as well as loving and caring for the children, I'm comfortable setting boundaries and rules. I think that I might have taken things more slowly if the kids were living between households and another parent had been actively involved.

Discipline is a tricky area for any parent, but I think it's harder for a stepparent. If you don't already have parenting experience, you might feel unsure of yourself when it comes to making rules and enforcing boundaries. Your sensitivity to your stepkids' feelings, especially if they've been through a lot of disruption, is also going to make you hesitant.

My number one piece of advice would be to talk to your partner and keep talking to them as you negotiate this rocky road. You two need to work together as a team and, if other parents are actively involved in the children's lives, ideally you'll all be able to come together and agree strategies going forward.

SETTING GROUND RULES
PROFESSOR LISA DOODSON

If there's another parent who's still involved, you don't always have control. You think you've got a plan and it gets taken away – perhaps they might have the children some of the time or want them for the holidays. It's hard, but the most important thing is to get your routine and decide with your partner what works for you.

You've got to set up how you want to live in your family because, if you don't, you're forever living someone else's rules and you'll just feel resentful.

It will get easier, but you have to give it time and be kind to each other while you're in this process of creating your exciting new family. After a few years, you'll get that pattern right.

PARENTING STYLE

Did you know that there are at least four distinct parenting styles? Diana Baumrind is the psychologist who first identified these styles in 1967 and her classifications are still widely accepted today:

1. ***Authoritarian:*** This is the 'Because I said so' parenting style, where parents set the rules and there are punishments or consequences if the rules are broken, often without being properly explained. Authoritarian parenting is demanding and adult-centred. These parents are trying to instil social responsibility, independence and ambition in their children without giving them much room to be autonomous.

2. ***Authoritative:*** This is the 'Let's have a chat about it' parenting style, a more child-focused approach where parents set rules, guidelines and boundaries, but are open to discussing the reasons for the rules

and more likely to forgive their children when rules are broken or challenged. Authoritative parents tend to model themselves on teachers/counsellors as they try to teach their children the importance of social responsibility, self-reliance, achievement and co-operation.

3. ***Permissive:*** This is the 'Can't say no' parenting style, where parents don't expect their children to be mature enough to abide by rules or guidelines, and don't exert a lot of control. Permissive parents want to be friends with their children; they are child-centred, undemanding and accepting.

4. ***Uninvolved:*** This is the 'Do it yourself' parenting style, where parents cater for their children's basic needs but don't monitor or supervise their behaviour. Uninvolved parents are detached, undemanding and often unresponsive – and in some cases neglectful.

What parenting style do you have? It may be a mix of all four! Do you and your partner's parenting styles align?

Whichever style of parenting – or combination of styles – is prominent in your family, it's important to be as consistent as you can when communicating your approach to the children, so that they don't get confused or play you and your partner off against each other.

It's all about finding common ground and this consistency is important in any family, but especially so in a stepfamily, where one parent may feel they have less right to exert authority over the children, at least in the early years.

DIFFERENT APPROACHES

No stepfamily is alike! Everything depends on who is on board with the new family structure – who is supportive, who is obstructive and if there's someone who just doesn't understand. Here's what I've gathered while speaking to other parents within the Blended community …

Stepparents without bio kids

For me, it's really important that all of my kids are treated the same, so if that means disciplining them all in the same way so it's fair, that's what I'll do.

This didn't come naturally at first – it took a while. Initially, there were things Rio and I didn't agree on, and merging two different homes with two different ideas of how to do things can be really tricky. It's about you and your partner talking about the set of standards you want in your home – the skills you want your children to develop as well as the adults you want them to grow into – and then working backwards from that.

Tip: **It's not about what we do for our kids, but what we teach them to do for themselves, like teaching those life skills they get annoyed about when you ask them – things like emptying the dishwasher and wiping the table.**

Feeling judged is almost as bad as feeling unwanted – and I felt there was a bit of both when I started out on this journey. I was conscious that some people felt offended if I corrected the children, because I'm not their biological mum, and I felt

I couldn't tell them off in front of certain people because they would judge me. It was all a bit sensitive and emotional, but it's better now that I feel fully confident in my role. I know that I'm the children's stepmum and I will do everything a mother does to support them and look after them and, at times, that also means disciplining them. Sometimes I still feel judged, which may be down to my own insecurities, but whereas five years ago, I might not have been able to deal with it, now I try to just brush it off. What's important is that the kids know I'm their stepmum and I'm not trying to replace their mum, but we are still all one.

If, like me, you come into an already-made family and you don't have children of your own, when it comes to discipline, another approach is to take your lead initially from your partner. Have discussions before you move in together about how to roll out your approach and agree to back each other up.

Some stepparents start off a bit like babysitters or childminders – they remind their stepchildren of rules, but don't act as an enforcer. Instead, they'll warn them that they'll be reporting misbehaviour to the bio parent. They need their partner to back them up when this happens, otherwise they will lose any authority they have.

Once they've built up respect, the 'babysitter' stepparent can move out of carer mode and become more of a parent to the children, with more parental leverage. It's easy to think, 'I can't be bothered ...' and relax the rules with them, but it's worth remembering that, in general, children respond better to firm but loving parenting rather than a more permissive anything-goes approach.

Stepparents with bio kids

What happens if there's a culture clash between your kids and your partner's when it comes to discipline? Or if your kids are used to living by different rules and boundaries from your partner's kids? It might be tempting to sit down with your partner, agree a new, shared set of rules and instantly start to enforce them. But both sets of kids have already had enough disruption – be it bereavement, divorce, moving home, moving schools, new siblings or new parent figures – so it might be worth letting everybody do things their way in the beginning, for a while at least. Give everyone time to settle into the new home and family structure; stay open to what's working and what's not with both sets of kids as you slowly blend. Check in with your partner regularly so that you feel confident that you're on the same page – and, if change needs to happen, make sure you take everybody with you.

If you're blending two sets of children, it might be a good idea for you and your partner to agree on a set of rewards and consequences that apply equally to all the children and to communicate these to the children so that they know where they stand.

When you don't approve of your partner's approach

Parenting is rarely straightforward, even when you welcome a baby together and work out what to do as you go along. It's definitely more complicated when you join an already-made family, with half-grown children, and your partner has already developed their style of parenting.

Unless your partner is living in chaos and finding it hard to cope, the children will probably not take kindly to a stranger telling them how things will be from now on. It's easy to want respect instantly, but, as we all know, it takes time to gain that. The best way I've found to do this is by showing you're trustworthy, reliable and predictable – and by demonstrating very clearly that the children's welfare and happiness is your priority. So even if you disagree with the way your partner parents, it's best not to wade in immediately and try to change things.

Don't forget that your partner knows the children way better than you do. As you get to know them, you may understand why they take a certain approach. Like anything, it takes time to get to know someone and why they act the way they do – the more you talk and understand what the kids have been through, the more you'll develop a bond. It's a process of getting to know each other.

HOW TO DISCUSS DISCIPLINE WITH YOUR PARTNER
LOUISE ALLEN

You might have different ideas on how to discipline or parent the kids, but if you have the children's best interests at the heart, you will be able to agree on discipline that works for your family. If the children's interests genuinely come first, there is less opportunity for grievances. Negative behaviour and poor boundaries do not help children thrive.

» Talk openly and freely and act with positive consistency. It's important to know and understand what went on before and how effective or ineffective those ideas were.

» Do not be afraid to talk to your partner about creating boundaries and consequences for your children. If you are scared to do this, I would suggest that there may still be issues that need to be discussed.

» Get in early. If you feel a child's behaviour is heading in the wrong direction, you need to nip it in the bud.

» Be observant and aware of your child. Know what's going on for them and talk to them and your partner.

» Avoid being overcritical. Your feelings about the child's behaviour may well be about you coming to terms with your own need to control your new life. Ask yourself, 'Does it matter?' Sometimes we just need to let it go.

I can be strict as a parent, but it's more with the little things like keeping your room tidy, not having your phone at the table, being on time and making sure you're ready for school the next day. The kids say I'm like the CID – nothing slips past me, which is very annoying for them! I'm the nagger – I nag constantly (I'm even fed up with the sound of my own voice!). I also overthink everything and worry that I've done the wrong thing. I'm extra sensitive, but I think that's just a feature of being a stepparent. I worry the kids are going to hate me.

It's hard when the family has a set way of doing things and then a new person comes in and tries to change it. In the early days, I found it difficult to pull the children up on things I didn't think were acceptable. When I moved in, the kids were allowed to play football in the house. I came along and didn't

agree with that. But, honestly, how do you tell a family of foot-
ballers that they can't kick a ball about in the house? And now
even Cree has started doing it – I'm going to have to change
the rules before something gets broken! I love seeing the kids
play football because it's their passion, but, I'm sorry, it's just
not an inside activity.

It's taken time, but now the kids know what is right and
wrong for our family, they know when I'm going to pull them
up on something and I feel so much more confident doing so.
It's been hard enough doing this with just me and Rio in the
mix. I can only imagine what a minefield it is when there's a
third parent involved.

When the previous partner has another set of rules

Nothing is going to undermine your and your partner's
attempts to set boundaries more than the non-resident parent
ignoring, or deliberately flouting, those boundaries. Criticism
from the previous partner, especially if it's communicated via
the children, will also chip away at your authority and confidence. It's a common problem and one way to counter it is to
keep things very separate by saying, 'You may be allowed to do
it in your mum's/dad's house, but not in this house.' It's a pity
not to have an integrated approach, but if the other parent
lets the kids stay up until all hours and you don't agree with
that, there's not much you can do. You could try speaking to
them about it – or if that fails, perhaps you could bring it up
with their partner, if they have one. Alternatively, explain to
the children why it's in their interest to get enough sleep – and
hope that they'll listen.

If you parent by rewarding good behaviour, it can really
become hard when the non-resident parent interferes with

your system, either by buying treats you've already promised the children (for instance, you've said they can have new trainers if they complete a course and then the other parent buys the trainers before the course is done) or allowing behaviour that you and your partner have banned (for instance, going out on week nights in the lead up to exams). In order to maintain the framework of your deal, you're going to have to renegotiate with the kids, unfortunately. If possible, let the other parent know in advance of your agreements with the kids and ask them not to obstruct or pre-empt them.

HOW TO DISCIPLINE STEPKIDS WHEN THERE IS ANOTHER BIO PARENT INVOLVED
LOUISE ALLEN

» For discipline across households to work, all the adults involved need to put any previous issues with each other aside to collectively be the best parents that they can be.

» Define your expectations and boundaries and gently make them known to the other adults.

» Be aware of how you talk about the ex in front of your children. If children find a weakness in the adults' connections, they will exploit it or that weakness will manifest into hurt and pain for the children.

» Consequences are better than punishment. It's important to know the difference. A punishment feels like retribution (or vengeance) for a wrongful act. Consequences are usually natural or logical outcomes that result from one's behaviour. You can get children to want to behave better through effective consequences. A consequence might be a loss of a privilege until your child completes a task or behaves acceptably for a specified period of time (not too long).

PARENTING TOGETHER

All couples have disagreements, but it's destabilising for everyone if you argue in front of the children. It is fine to show vulnerability as an individual, but the two of you need to demonstrate that you're united. You are the bedrock of the family.

Research shows that kids perceive conflict between their parents as destabilising for the family unit, so it follows that they will feel much more relaxed if they see you and your partner as a united front, working closely to forge your new family structure. That doesn't mean they won't feel resentful sometimes, or act out their fears and worries, or try to challenge or undermine the relationship. (I know! It's a lot!) Try to work together as a unit through the rocky patches.

In the early days, when the kids were younger, Rio and I did our best to stay on the same page in front of the children. Whatever happened, we tried to act as one even if we didn't necessarily agree. Later, when the kids weren't around, we'd talk it through.

Now that the boys are older, Rio and I speak more openly in front of them – sometimes we have a full-on bicker. That means that if we do slightly disagree, it's fine because there's more of an open forum to talk it through.

I've heard about situations where the biological parent says to their partner, 'Well, I'm their dad/mum and you're not.' I wouldn't accept that. I'm quite a fiery person and I put all my love, energy and time into the kids and I'd want to be seen as an equal in all aspects of parenting.

SOMETIMES THE KIDS KNOW MORE ...

As an adult, you normally know more than a child knows, or at least you feel it should be that way. But it's often not the case when you first move in with an already-made family. You find yourself in a position where the kids know a lot more about the workings of your new household than you do.

So you say, 'Come on, bath time,' and they reply, 'No, we have a bath in the morning.'

You can't get hold of your partner. 'Well, I think you should have one now,' you say.

'But we always have one in the morning.'

'Oh, OK, well …'

It's a potentially awkward situation – trust me, I've been there! So, what do you do? As a stepparent, you need to be quick, clear and decisive at times, just like any parent. If it turns out to be the wrong call, I'd say, 'Listen, guys, my mistake, but you're clean now anyway, so it's fine.'

In the beginning, I didn't like to show too much weakness because I thought the children might take advantage of that. It's clear that they did know more than me about the routine as I was new to the family and, sometimes, they'd tell little fibs, so it was all about trying to work out what was true and what wasn't! It's inevitable that kids will tell small fibs sometimes and play you off against one another. Sometimes they even do it just to keep everyone happy and not cause any upset.

It can be hard, though, when they tell one story to you and another to your partner and you feel a bit caught in the middle.

HOW TO DEAL WITH DISHONESTY IN KIDS
DR DOMINIQUE THOMPSON

People lie for lots of different reasons, and children will lie to avoid conflict or punishment, or because they believe that their decision-making is right and their parent's is wrong, for example, about how they should dress or behave. Teens in particular will prioritise their peers' opinions and spending time with friends, which could also potentially drive dishonest behaviour. If teens are being dishonest, it is always worth starting with the 'why' of the situation and not assuming the worst.

Try to stay calm, discuss what has happened and hear their side of the story. Explain your concerns. If they are your stepchildren and they have behaved in an unacceptable way, you may need to discuss what you are worried about with their bio parent. Be open and honest with children wherever possible. Role model the behaviour you expect from them. Explain why you are worried and keep communicating with them.

You can't really fully prepare for these moments – there are always going to be things you don't know and, until you're settled and secure, issues will pop up. There's no getting away from the fact that, with four children now, I'm outnumbered!

I had daughters and I had to build my confidence when it came to disciplining my teenage stepsons – and I think my partner felt the same about it with my girls. It took a while for the boys to trust me and respect my authority as a parent, but now we have a great relationship.

Discipline gets easier if you constantly communicate and have a lot of patience. Also, try not to focus on the negatives. Teenagers are hard work, but they do get better. One of the boys was 13 when my partner and I met and he was pretty awful, but now he is a wonderful young man. One of the girls wasn't particularly nice to be around about a year ago, but seems a lot happier now. At the moment, my youngest daughter is the one who is really testing us. Knowing that it is just a phase really helps us on the bad days and knowing that I have my partner's support and encouragement is everything.

ZOE, BLENDED FAMILY OF SIX

SAYING SORRY

I always own up to my mistakes. The children didn't know that in the beginning, but they do now. If I've told the kids off and then realise I was wrong, I'm definitely not against admitting it: 'You know what? I'm sorry, maybe I was a bit harsh; I didn't mean it exactly like that. I meant it like this. I shouldn't have said or done this instead. I'm just feeling a bit overwhelmed today.'

If something's gone wrong, it's important to talk about it. It's a way for children to learn that you're not perfect and that it's OK to be imperfect and wrong sometimes.

Seeing me say sorry has taught the kids to do the same when they're in the wrong. In the last couple of years, I've seen the children admitting when they're in the wrong, which is great.

Tip: **It's OK to show that we don't really know exactly what we're doing and we're working on it. It gives us all space to be imperfect.**

THE IMPORTANCE OF BOUNDARIES

Boundaries are really important for children and for the whole family to know where everyone stands. Although it can be difficult to set boundaries, especially as a stepparent, it makes things easier in the long run as everyone knows the standards we expect as a family.

They may not think they do, but children thrive on boundaries and they react really well to them. I've found that having a safe, solid structure works well for them. Some parents enforce boundaries by being strict and laying down the law; others instil values through repetition and modelling.

A lot of stepparents I know have tried setting house rules, with different outcomes and degrees of success. I think it's just a positive to be having those conversations. But I know that, for some people, having a more formal family chat really helps. Here are some tips from the Blended community on making it work:

» Before you start, have a conversation with your partner and agree on fundamental house rules. Think about areas where you struggle or there's conflict. Make a list.

FAMILY
House Rules

1.

2.

3.

4.

5.

6.

7.

8.

9.

10.

» Gather together and set out some guidelines for the meeting. For instance, no interrupting while someone else is speaking.

» Start by explaining that the meeting is about helping your family to be happy, healthy and positive. It's about life running as smoothly as possible for everybody who lives in your home. Family comes first.

» Go through the initial list you made with your partner, putting a tick against rules that everybody agrees are non-negotiable. Safety and kindness are top priorities for many families.

» Make sure everyone understands that both adults have equal authority. The parents are in charge and the stepparent has as much right to expect rules to be obeyed as a biological parent.

» Ask everyone to say one thing they can't stand (shoes in the kitchen, being tickled, pinched or licked by a sibling, wet towels on the bedroom floor, saying, 'Whatever' or 'Shut up' ... or footballs being kicked around inside the house – lol!).

» Listen to the children's views, especially when they explain an alternative way of doing things or mention something they're allowed to do when they're with their other parent or were permitted to do in the past.

» Decide whether household chores should be on the list. What happens when chores are left undone?

» Don't make the list of rules too long. You can add to it later.

» House rules should be achievable because, if they're not, they will instantly be broken and soon forgotten, much to your frustration. Respect, honesty, truth, trust and keeping your word are all reasonable expectations.

» Write down the main points, type them up in a friendly font/colour and pin them up somewhere visible, like the fridge door.

WORKING OUT HOUSE RULES
LOUISE ALLEN

When parenting across households, it is helpful if the households share similar house rules. Keep them simple and achievable, such as 'speak with kindness', 'knock on bedroom doors before you enter' and – my absolute favourite – 'you are responsible for your own mess; leave the loo as others would want to find it'. Try not to make it a long list otherwise you will tire and fail at upholding the rules.

When it comes to house rules, there is a sign in our hallway that says it all:

Love one another.
Say please and thank you.
Give hugs and kisses.
If you drop it, pick it up.
Eat your greens.
If you open it, close it.

Dream big.
Laugh, learn, share, smile, forgive.
Share chocolate.
Play nice, work hard.
No whining.
If you turn it on, turn it off.
Be honest.

Saying all of this, I still walk into my kids' rooms and find their clothes scattered all over the floor and the drawers left open, but it's a work in progress!

HOW TO NAVIGATE HOUSE RULES WITH YOUR PARTNER'S EX
PROFESSOR LISA DOODSON

If you have the children a lot of the time but feel that the other bio partner is always in control, it's about setting boundaries. When the children are with you, what's important and what do you want to do? It's about talking to your partner and, if you've got into a routine where the ex is always setting the expectations of what you can and can't do, it's about pushing back a bit into what's reasonable.

» Pick your battles. Sometimes it's worth letting some things go so that you can focus on the things that really matter to you.

» Ask yourself why you don't feel in control – is it that someone else is stopping you or is it just yourself?

> » Take things slowly and establish one change at a
> time. Work out what causes the most stress in the
> household and focus on making small changes that
> can make a real difference.
>
> » Everything takes longer to establish in a household
> where the children only live part of the time. You
> might have to keep reminding the children of
> boundaries or your house rules!

DEALING WITH OVERWHELM

*'When you react, you let others control you.
When you respond, you are in control.'*

BOHDI SANDERS, BESTSELLING AUTHOR,
MARTIAL ARTIST AND LIFE COACH

Sometimes patience will elude you and everything will get to
be too much, especially if someone's having a row. My advice,
if you're feeling overwhelmed in the moment, is to try taking
yourself to a quiet place. If that's not possible, standing still
and inhaling deeply gives you *breathing space* and helps to raise
your patience levels. Shutting your eyes and silently counting
to ten will help – and some people clench and release their fists
a certain number of times.

In the space you've created for yourself, identify how you
are feeling and try to detach yourself emotionally.

This is a difficult one, because although everybody might
be angry, for example, each person's anger may be rooted

in a different interpretation of what is actually going on. For instance:

Your stepchild does an activity after agreeing
with you to clear up afterwards,
but instead leaves a big mess.

You are angry because of the mess (and anxious that
your stepchild doesn't respect you enough to clear up).

Your stepchild is angry that you are the one telling
them off rather than their bio parent (and worried
that it means you won't like them).

Your partner is angry that their child
won't accept your parental authority
(and feels guilty about the whole situation).

It's complicated!

Remind yourself that countless other people have experienced similar predicaments and complex emotions and feelings. Take comfort from the knowledge that your feelings, the issue or conflict will pass.

I read a quote recently about how difficult it is when you feel rejected by a child who you've showered with love and energy, and how it's not really about you. Instinctively knowing this, a bio parent finds it easier to brush it off, but a stepparent tends to blame themselves and look for reasons why they have earned the child's rejection. I think there's a lot of truth in this because I always question myself as a stepparent and think that everything that doesn't go to plan or the kids' negative reactions are because of what I'm doing wrong. With my stepkids, I always think, 'Oh no, what have I done?' whereas with Cree, I don't have the same insecurity. I just don't feel as stressed about him in the same way and I'm not sure why. When you're a stepparent, you add extra pressure to yourself and assume that any hostility you encounter is because you're not doing something right. But they're just kids. If I think with my logical brain, all parents find parenting difficult, but when you're in the moment with all the emotions, it's hard to see this. This is when tapping into your emotional intelligence can help.

DEVELOPING YOUR EMOTIONAL INTELLIGENCE

CARLY KEEN

Our journey into the blended family community was not a smooth one. For the first few years, we were all still experiencing big emotions surrounding our situation. I was plagued with anxiety whenever the phone would ring or a text would come through.

Three years into my relationship with my partner, while I was working in a tutor-based role in schools, I came across the concept of emotional intelligence (EQ). I realised that EQ could help both my students who were really struggling to recognise and manage their emotions within the classroom and, with my own deteriorating mental health, developing my EQ was key to helping me manage my big emotions around my partner's ex.

Having learned and taught a simple age-accessible way to understand what happens in our brain when we experience overwhelming emotions, I was able to understand where my anxiety was coming from. Typically, when our brain senses a threat, it will be the 'downstairs' primitive part of our brain that reacts. My anxiety was in overdrive because I believed that something bad would happen every time we were in contact with my partner's ex. It was an extreme overreaction based on what we had all experienced over the previous few years.

Learning about the brain and strategies to help engage our 'upstairs' rational and calm brain meant that I could put it into practice straightaway. As soon as I felt any stirrings of big emotions, I would implement the following strategies:

» Taking ten deep breaths.

» Filling my mind with things I was grateful for.

» Naming the emotions as they came up.

I knew that each time I could effectively recognise and manage those emotions, I was building new connections in my brain. This was reshaping how my brain was accessing 'the threat of the ex', which ultimately wasn't threatening at all.

This was transformative for my own mental health and my family's. I felt more in control of my emotions and also responsible for them. Developing my EQ has meant that

I now take ownership of my emotions. No one else can make you feel a certain way. We choose how we respond in every situation. And that is where our power lies.

I have gone on to set up my own business helping children and parents develop their EQ, which very simply is the ability to recognise and then manage big emotions. It has helped me to become more resilient and empathic, particularly to those who are obviously struggling themselves, and it's my goal to create generational change in how we express our emotions and parent our children.

Rules change as kids get older and sometimes boundaries relax, but discipline is always important. Everybody needs to know what's allowed and not allowed at home and within the family.

Right from the start, it was important to me and Rio that we encouraged respect within the household. His support was crucial with this because getting the children to listen to me was just so difficult at first. They didn't want to listen; they didn't really know me at that stage and they'd play up whenever they felt they could. Looking back, I don't actually know when this changed and, don't get me wrong, they can still be difficult sometimes, but I guess with time we just got to know each other more, our relationship formed and that helped us have mutual respect for each other. I hope that you can also find your way as a blended family through the minefield that is discipline.

CHAPTER 6

DEALING WITH AWKWARD MOMENTS

'I am thankful for my struggle because, without it, I wouldn't have stumbled across my strength.'

There still seems to be a large section of society that expects a family to fit a conventional template, but blended families come in so many different shapes and forms. Those of us with more complex situations often have some explaining to do when it comes to our kids, wider family, friends, acquaintances and strangers.

There's scope for a lot of embarrassing and awkward moments in the life of a stepparent, especially when you don't fit other people's idea of what a family looks like. Ex-partners and other family members can also throw spanners in the works. In this chapter, I'm here to warn you about the things that can go wrong so that you don't make some of the mistakes I've made.

When these awkward situations pop up, they're always difficult, but hopefully with these tips you'll be able to prepare yourself a little better.

OUT AND ABOUT

'Are they your kids?' 'How many children do you have?' 'Are you their mum?' Oh, those dreaded questions! I always really struggled when I first got asked these and, though people probably didn't mean to upset me or make me anxious, they always did. Even now, I can be very tetchy around this subject.

Although I'm not their biological mum, I still call Lorenz, Tate and Tia my kids; with Cree, I am a mum of four. I have four children. If you suggest that I have one, I will correct you. If you treat one of them differently to the other three, I will also have a big problem – I believe all four of the children should be treated equally.

If you ask if I am their mum, I will say that I am their stepmum and, although they are not biologically mine, I still see them as my children. In our house, the children are treated as one. It's my job to nurture and care for them and make sure they are given all the love they deserve. Sometimes other people don't see it that way, though.

Questions like this may keep popping up in public and it's inevitable that when you're out and about, people will refer to you as the kids' mum or dad – 'I've just given it to your mum', 'You and your dad can come in now'. This can sometimes feel a bit uncomfortable – it's kind of like the elephant in the room – and it takes a lot of energy to correct people, so there may be times when you just let it go. But it's important that you've had a private conversation with your partner and the kids about these potential situations and agree on what would work best for you all as a family. This way, when anyone asks again, you will all feel more comfortable.

Having said that, you can't prepare for every situation. The other day a delivery driver came to the house to deliver something and said to the kids, 'The last time I was here, I was delivering your mum's wedding dress.'

The kids looked at me and said, 'I don't know who he's talking about. Is it you? Or is it Mum?'

It's just awkward, isn't it?

AT THE AIRPORT

Before I became a stepmum, I didn't know that you can't travel with children if you don't share the same surname. I just assumed that if you're their parent, you can travel with them. Unfortunately, I learned this the hard way when I took the children on holiday – Rio had left a day earlier – and the officials at passport control started asking questions because I was travelling with minors who didn't share my surname. It was a bit emotional for us all and I couldn't wait to get out of there.

When I think about this logically, it makes complete sense because if a child was being smuggled out of the country, I'd want them to be stopped, but I just didn't think about it because I see them as my kids – and having to explain myself made me even more aware that, on paper, people don't see us as a family.

'The last names may not match, but the hearts certainly do.'

Tip: **Be aware that each country has different requirements when travelling with a minor with a different surname, so make sure that you check this before travelling. From my experience, you'll normally need a letter of authorisation signed by the bio parent along with a copy of their passport, but each country differs.**

AT THE DOCTOR'S

As a stepparent, you naturally fall into doing lots of different things for your kids – like booking appointments or taking them to the doctor's. You don't think about it too much as you're just doing what you need to do.

However, I often find myself in situations where questions are asked that I just can't answer. It is normally something that happened before I was in the children's lives: 'Have they had chicken pox?' 'Did they have all their immunisations as a baby?'

I freeze and think, 'Shit, I don't bloody know!' An awkward, embarrassed feeling comes over me, and reality sets in. Am I being judged? I should know this! How do I not?

Starting my journey as a childless stepmum, these are things that had never crossed my mind, which in itself brings on more guilt as I could sometimes feel really embarrassed that I didn't know the things a parent should. This may sound silly, as really it's impossible to know every single detail when you have not parented a child from birth.

Now that our medical histories have been digitalised and are accessible to parents and carers who have permission to look at them, it's a lot easier to prepare yourself before you go to the doctor or hospital with one of your stepchildren. One way to help yourself remember which illnesses and ailments each child has had is to ask them, your partner or other relatives what they recall about the children's experiences of being ill, and if there were any puzzling, worrying or emergency moments. Chicken pox, high fevers, broken bones, strange rashes and digestive disasters become memorable if they're told to you as stories. Alternatively, write a list of bullet points and carry a photo of it on your phone.

I used to put so much pressure on myself to know absolutely everything so that I wouldn't be caught out in certain situations, but as time has gone on, I'm beginning to realise this is just not possible and I am no less of a parent for not knowing everything.

I'm really trying to work on being less hard on myself, but it's a work in progress as sometimes, when I'm caught off guard, these things that might seem like tiny details to others just magnify the situation we are in.

I am a sensitive soul and sometimes that frustrates me, but I believe that sensitivity is also my strength as it enables me to be the loving, caring person I am, who can see past blood and genetics and truly love without limitations.

AT THE HOSPITAL

In everyday life, I constantly make decisions for the kids – whether it's what we're doing at the weekend, what they're wearing or what we're having for dinner. So, in an emergency, I'd always want to be there for the kids too. When you're used to making all these decisions and being so involved in your children's lives, it can take you by surprise when you're questioned by medical professionals – say in A&E – whether you're 'Mum' or 'Dad'. When you say 'No' and they ask where the kids' mum or dad are, it makes you feel inadequate and that you shouldn't be there. I don't think people do it on purpose – they're just unaware – and it plays into the roles that society has created for stepparents.

Added to my awkwardness is the way these questions make the kids feel. In times of hurt, children are vulnerable, so these questions are only causing more pain when they're already hurting. It would be so much better if, in this day and age, as a matter of course, professionals could ask, 'What's your relationship to the child?' rather than automatically assuming you're the biological parent. A lot of feelings would be spared that way!

To prepare yourself:

» Go in with proof of who you are.

» Have a consent letter from the bio parent and keep it on your phone.

» Be prepared that you might be quizzed and have the answers ready so you feel more in control.

> *I remember when my eldest was in secondary school, I'd signed the consent form for her to have a vaccination and the school had to ring up and gain consent from my husband because, for them, I wasn't able to 'provide consent'. This still sticks with me – I felt like screaming down the phone at them that I am my stepdaughter's 24/7 mum; I do everything a parent does ... what more do I need to do?! But I knew it wouldn't do any good. It's small things like that – things you don't really think of – that have the power to stop you in your tracks, destroy confidence and make you feel completely useless.*
>
> ROSIE, STEPMUM OF TWO

PARENTAL RESPONSIBILITY
LAURA NASER

In law, whether cohabiting with a biological parent or married to a biological parent, it does not automatically provide that adult with any rights or responsibilities to the child. Often, the partner of a biological parent can play a very significant role in the child's life and be viewed for all intents and purposes by the child as another parent, and yet they are not in law treated as one just by virtue of having a parental-like role in the child's life.

'Parental responsibility' is the legal term used to refer to parental rights, responsibilities and duties for a child, and includes (but is not limited to):

» The name by which the child is known.

» Removing the child from the country (even for a short break).

» Giving permission for them to receive medical treatment.

» Their education.

» Their religious upbringing.

» Administering the child's property and financial affairs.

The inability to consent to a child receiving medical treatment or to take them abroad are probably the two that stand out the most as potential issues for a non-biological parent. Any non-biological parent, even if they have been in the child's life for some time and are viewed as a psychological and social parent to that child, cannot legally take that child outside of the country, even for a day trip, without the written consent of those who do have parental responsibility for the child. Likewise, if the child requires medical attention, they cannot legally provide their consent for it.

It is possible for those with parental responsibility for a child (do note that while it is automatically given to a birth mother, parental responsibility is not always automatically acquired by the biological father) to enter into a parental responsibility agreement with a non-biological parent. This does not remove parental responsibility from the other parents. If the biological parents with parental responsibility do not both consent to the agreement, then an application to the court for a parental responsibility order can be made by the non-biological parent, but for this specific application they must be a stepparent, i.e. married to one of the biological parents who has parental responsibility for the child. For those who are unmarried, they would need a Child Arrangements Order, which orders that the child either spends time with them or lives with them (even partially and along with a biological parent) to gain parental responsibility.

Another important point to consider is what would happen if the biological parent died. The children would most likely live with the surviving biological parent and the stepparent would not automatically have a continuing relationship with the children. In this scenario, an application to the court for a Child Arrangements Order would be necessary (assuming one did not already exist), and the court would need to consider whether it would be in the children's best interest to allow the non-biological parent to spend time with the children or have them live with them (even for just some of their time).

AT SCHOOL

At some point, the biological parent needs to let the children's school know about changes to the family situation. This will make parents' evenings, school fetes and pick-ups easier and less awkward for everyone.

This didn't happen for me! I went to pick up the kids from school one day and I was questioned. Not only was I so nervous about that first pick-up and being judged, getting stopped made me feel even more like an imposter. As silly as it sounds, we didn't even think about telling the school because the kids knew me so well and we were already forming a new family unit together.

Again, it makes complete sense that people are challenged when picking up kids from school – I wouldn't ever want a stranger to pick up my kids – but it's just another lesson I learned coming to the family as a childless stepparent.

Here are some tips to help you avoid the same situation:

» Get your partner to speak to your stepchild's teacher or welfare officer at the school or, if this isn't possible, send a clear, factual email to the school office, head teacher, head of year or form teacher explaining the situation and any concerns they might have within the school setting.

» You could also ask to be addressed in a particular way – say, not as a mum/mummy – if it's appropriate, to avoid being miscalled at pick-up and drop-off.

» Have a conversation with your stepkids to help prepare them for questions or teasing they may experience at school – for instance, about the new family structure, additional siblings or moving home or area. These changes may well attract more attention from the children's peers, but they should be fine as long as they have answers ready.

Having an open dialogue with the school is helpful for the children as well. The school should really know if there's a breakdown in their parents' relationship or if students are settling into a new family structure, because these sorts of changes can make children behave in different ways. The school may pick up on changes that are not so apparent at home and, if a student suddenly starts playing up in class, their behaviour changes or they appear withdrawn or depressed, teachers will have more of an idea of why these things might be happening.

At the start, there was a lot of push back from the kids, who would say things like, 'You're not my dad'. This manifested in them playing up at school, acting out all their strong emotions. We worked closely with the school to support them and, over time, we've all slotted into the new set-up and the behaviour issues have calmed down.

RAHUL, BLENDED FAMILY OF SIX

COMMUNICATING WITH YOUR CHILD'S SCHOOL

LAURA HERMAN

I remember counselling a young person struggling with his behaviour in school. His parents had maintained a good relationship with each other, even though they were going through a divorce. They were really surprised to find out that he was upset about them splitting up and that their break-up had impacted on his behaviour in school. They had wrongly assumed he was fine because they had maintained a good relationship with each other. It is important to notice changes in a child's behaviour, and a good flow of information between you and the child's school can sometimes help to highlight what isn't always visible to a parent.

Tip: **Always let your younger stepkids know in advance when you are going to pick them up from school or a friend's party to minimise the chances of them shouting, 'No, I don't want you – I want Mummy/Daddy!'**

WITHIN THE FAMILY

If you're told by a child something that another family member has said about you that isn't nice, it's natural to want to defend yourself, but sometimes it's best just not to get into it. Here's an example:

If it's coming from someone else in the family, I would always try to make excuses and say, 'Oh, they're just upset.

They shouldn't really be saying that because it's not very nice, but we have to give them a break because they've been through a lot. Do you want me to talk to them for you? What do you want me to do? As long as we are nice, that is all that matters.'

When you're being compared, it's sometimes hard to be the bigger person and speak fondly of the family member like this, but in the long run, it's better for everyone involved, especially the children.

If it's a serious issue, then you have to sit down and talk, bearing in mind that it can be hard to navigate because children tell their version of the truth.

A lot of adults put their pain on to the children, which isn't healthy. A child of a young age doesn't understand why parents or a family member should be horrible or rude. 'I just want everyone to love me; why are they doing this?'

I spoke to Professor Lisa Doodson on how to deal with an ex-partner who says negative things about the stepparent to the child. This is what she had to say:

EXPERT VIEW
PROFESSOR LISA DOODSON

It's so sad when this happens, and it happens more than we'd like to think. It's about keeping the moral high ground and not getting involved. Children will work it out eventually. If you treat the children the way you've always treated them and care for them consistently when they come to stay, they'll eventually realise it's the other person who is making these things up. It can take time and that's the hard part, but if you get in a battle of trying to defend yourself, it becomes very difficult for the children to understand who to believe and what to think. It's also difficult putting a child into a loyalty bind – children will usually try to defend other family members, especially their bio parent, and this can be really difficult for a stepparent to hear when they know what they're saying is just not true!

Change the subject if the children bring it up. They will often appreciate it if you cut those conversations short – they don't want, or need, to deal with conflict. The other person needs to go through their own journey and this can take time. Try to minimise those conversations and not dwell on it. Make sure your partner always supports you and remind yourself that it will get easier as the other person begins to move on with their own life.

This works well for younger children, but once they're a bit older, I think it's important to sit down with them and try to explain how everyone's feeling without badmouthing anyone.

It is difficult to get past people's opinions and it's hard not to just give up. From my personal experience, coming from a broken home, I just don't think it's healthy to be the person who speaks badly of another person, whether that is the biological parent, the ex's family or whoever. I try to be that fair, positive person as much as I can because I don't feel like a child should take on that burden of worry. We shouldn't be giving our children more worry – we should be taking their worry away.

> *The children often tell me things that their mum has said to them about how I parent or that I am not capable of looking after five children. Sometimes I hear it myself while they're on FaceTime to her in the living room. My husband spoke to her about it and asked her to stop, but she won't. So I just have to be the better person and prove by my actions that she's wrong.*

NICOLE, BLENDED FAMILY OF SEVEN

DIFFICULT QUESTIONS

As a stepparent, you might be faced with questions like, 'Why have you come to live with us?' or 'Do you love my dad/mum?' When you're faced with difficult questions like this from a child, I think you have to put your feelings and ego to one side. It's inevitable that they're going to wonder what's going on.

I always try to be honest with my answers, without overloading the child with unnecessary information. As an example, if your stepchild asks you, 'Are you trying to replace my mum?' you could answer with something along the lines of: 'Your mummy's amazing and I would never, ever want to take away from what she does. I am here when you are with Daddy just to give you some extra love when Mummy's not here. That doesn't mean that I am taking over from Mummy because she is amazing. Mummy and Daddy are still your mum and dad, but I can love you too.'

Tip: **If they ask a question that you can't immediately answer, give yourself time to think through what you want to say. Try answering with, 'That's a really good question. Let me think about it …'**

I'm not sure these questions ever stop coming, but the more comfortable you become in your position and the more you build a bond with your stepchildren, the easier they will be to answer.

ALWAYS REMEMBER ...

SOPHIE RANTZAU

It's not that children automatically hate the stepparent because they're the wicked witch or ogre. It's actually the child dealing with the huge change of their parents separating and the loss that comes with one parent no longer being in their life in the same capacity they were previously. How we slot this other person – the new stepparent – into their new life and what that looks like for the child makes all the difference, whether they're 12 or 25 or 45.

FACING DOWN THE GREEN-EYED MONSTER

Feelings around your partner can be complicated for everyone, especially at the start of your blended journey – but also going forward. You are sharing them with the children and at times this may make both sides feel jealous or excluded. It might surprise you to think that you could be jealous of your stepchildren, but if you find yourself in competition with them for their parent's attention, you could easily feel resentful at times. I've heard from quite a few stepparents who feel this way. Probably all of us have felt it once or twice.

The best way around this is to put yourself in the children's shoes and see things from their point of view. You can't blame them for thinking you're getting in the way of their relationship with their parent, which in any case may feel less secure than it did before their first family splintered. A lot will depend on what happened before you came along and how much they know or sense of that, but the chances are that at first they will feel possessive of your partner and distrustful of you – and they may also be hyper-alert to how their other parent or family members feel about you.

Does your partner feel torn between you and the children, or expect you to sort out your feelings and the children's without their help? It's really important to have conversations about how to bond your family. Every family faces challenges and it's up to you and your partner to find solutions together, whenever possible. Stay connected and keep talking! Reassure each other of your love.

HOW TO NAVIGATE FAMILY DYNAMICS
DR EMMA SVANBERG

One of the many tricky things about family life is the way that relationships within families can move between different alliances. It is easy for family members to feel excluded, especially if there are relationships that seem to be smoother than others. This is something to be mindful of as we form new family relationships. We might form alliances based on shared interests or experiences, but when these alliances begin to exclude someone else, this can cause difficult situations; a process called 'triangulation' (essentially where two sides of a triangle are pulling together to shut out the third!). This can happen between parents, or between adults and children.

It can feel like a very difficult situation, but it can help to look at the fear which is underlying that need to close ranks. And often that is a question which sounds something like, 'Does this person really love me?' or even 'Can this person love someone else and still love me?' This doesn't only happen in blended families, of course; it happens in all families when children realise that we have relationships outside of our relationship with them.

The first step when triangulation is beginning to occur is to offer reassurance – or it may be that you are the person feeling rejected, in which case you might need to offer yourself some reassurance. Families can be messy and complicated, and this might not be what you imagined!

The second step is to make sure that you keep the walls of that triangle sturdy, allowing discord to occur, as it inevitably will, but being able to keep all of the connections going in the family, even when people aren't getting on. What that might look like in principle might be, for example, a child saying 'See, she hates me!' to your new partner – inviting you as their parent to come into an alliance with them. When we are feeling guilty about bringing a change into our child's life, it's so easy to respond by swooping in to reassure them of our love … but this stops our new partner and child from being able to resolve this difference between them. Instead, we might step back, become curious about our child's feelings but work with our partner to resolve the situation – ensuring all three sides of the triangle feel not just strong, but well supported by each other.

DEALING WITH SPECIAL OCCASIONS

Anniversaries, birthdays and other special occasions are usually a time for happiness and celebration, but they can be a minefield for blended families.

In my situation, I want to include all the branches of the family in important events as much as possible, but other stepparents won't have this option and may find themselves being excluded. Often there's an agreement between separated parents to alternate occasions like Christmas, Easter and the children's birthdays, which can be painful in different ways for everyone.

It can be hard to have to share your children at Christmas and other special occasions. Here are some tips from the Blended community to get through it:

» Give the kids a second Christmas on another day – on Christmas Eve or Boxing Day or later in the month – and, of course, this also applies to Eid, Yom Kippur, Diwali, Chinese New Year and other special dates and holidays.

» Create your own traditions for your special blended occasion – these can include anything from serving up favourite foods to rituals around decorations or present-opening – and make sure everyone feels that it's an extra treat rather than the next best thing.

» If you haven't got your children on the big day, try to keep busy and make plans for yourself so you're not on your own.

» When the kids come home, be positive about their time with the other parent – ask questions and be curious.

» Try to arrange a video call at a convenient time for everyone so that you feel included and have some time with your kids on their special day.

» Handovers at this time of year can sometimes work better in a neutral place – in a shopping centre or at a supermarket car park. A quick hello is all that's needed, along with any information that needs to be shared about the children.

» Father Christmas could deliver presents to both homes, if the kids are split between households over Christmas. Both parents should have a conversation about presents (so as not to duplicate) and whether to set a limit on spending (to make it fair), either in person, by email and text or through co-parenting apps (see page 220).

Occasions like Christmas or children's birthdays are incredibly special and everyone wants to be present and take part. Try to put your own feelings aside and think about what and who is important on this occasion. What really matters is that your child or stepchild has a wonderful and memorable day – and who's to say that they won't have an even better time celebrating all over again with you at another point?

When trying to decide what to do for a milestone celebration, keep in mind the following:

» What is best for the children?

» What is best for your relationship?

» What is best for the short versus the long term?

I'm a number one worrier – I worry about the most minor of things sometimes – so when it comes to big events like anniversaries or birthdays, I can get myself in a right pickle. As parents, I think we worry about everything, but nine times out of ten, the worrying beforehand is worse than the actual event. I'm still working on trying not to put so much energy into the days leading up to these big occasions.

I find anniversaries particularly difficult; I feel like I don't know what to say or where I should be. I don't think it will ever get easier. It just really hits home the complexities of our family at these times.

If I'm working, I will normally just send a message letting them know that I am thinking of them (I go to work early, before school and college) and we don't really talk about it after that, which is probably the wrong way but it's the way it has been for years now. I suppose it's difficult, as I look at them as my children, but here we are celebrating a day to a parent who is no longer here. It's just strange.

Something I learned in therapy is that it's normal to feel resentment, jealousy, anger and hurt towards everybody involved within a stepfamily setting. Had I have known this all those years ago, I don't think I would have felt so

> *guilty for feeling all those things – I just thought I must be*
> *a really awful person for feeling that way when, in fact, it*
> *was completely and utterly normal.*
>
> *Thankfully, after nearly eight years, we are a very happy*
> *family, although tough times do crop up every now and*
> *then. I love them all so much and couldn't imagine my life*
> *any differently now – they are the best team I could ever*
> *have behind me.*

SIOBHAN, MUM OF ONE, STEPMUM OF TWO

Mother's and Father's Day

For most people, Mother's/Father's Day is a day when we celebrate the parents who shaped us. But, unfortunately, that is just not the case for everyone. For me personally, Mother's Day is a day that I struggle with. It's such a strange feeling, waking up and knowing that the whole country is celebrating this day, but my family is feeling a loss. I have a tendency to take on everyone's feelings and, in the lead up to the big day, I start worrying about Rio and the kids.

I struggled with Mother's Day even before I was a bio parent. I thought it might be easier when Cree was born, but actually, Mother's Day 2021 was the toughest to date. It was my first Mother's Day with my bio son – a day that, in another life, I would really look forward to – but how could I have the audacity to celebrate myself when all my family have experienced such a deep loss? I can't help but feel terrible guilt and I need to work on managing that. It seemed really selfish to me to want to be celebrated and I felt alone and quite isolated. I just didn't know anyone who was going through the same sort of thing as me.

I've since realised – through making the documentary, as well as meeting people through my podcast and social media accounts – that in fact there are so many people going through the same thing. I feel that a weight has been lifted off my shoulders and that I'm not alone. It's one of the reasons I started *Blended* – it really helps to lessen the load just knowing that you're not alone. When you can relate to someone who is going through a similar situation, you just feel better. If you can see people who are further along the journey than you, you can see that you're going to be OK and will get through this.

Mother's/Father's Day is a bloody hard day for lots of people. Here are my tips on supporting yourself through it:

- » Keep yourself occupied.

- » Spend time with people who love you.

- » Let your emotions out.

- » Don't be too harsh on yourself or expect too much of yourself.

- » Try to connect with people going through the same thing.

I asked psychotherapist Julia Samuel whether she had any tips on how to get through the day or even the build-up to it. This is what she had to say:

TIPS TO GET THROUGH THE DAY
JULIA SAMUEL, MBE

Allow yourself to feel what you're feeling: For those people whose parents have died, or who have lost a child, or have, for whatever reason, a complicated relationship with Mother's/Father's Day, it's so important to allow yourself to feel that loss. This often feels like fear, so allow yourself to name that: 'I'm feeling a bit fearful. I feel shaken and don't know what to do.' Often we turn against ourselves and feel we shouldn't be having certain feelings. By naming it, hopefully you can find a way of expressing it in some way – releasing some of the emotion, some of the tension. In doing so, that frees you up to have another feeling. Maybe you can trust a bit more, maybe you can allow yourself to both feel the pain of loss and the affection of and connection from love, and hold both feelings side by side. One feeling of loss doesn't knock out the feeling of love and hope. It's about letting yourself know that you feel this and that you can dare to live and love again.

Seek support from your family and friends: The key support that people need when they're grieving, whatever the loss, is the love and support of others, and it's hope that is the alchemy that turns a life around.

On these big days, everyone outpours their love on socials and it's all in the shops – it's everywhere. Sometimes I feel like coming off social media for the day. I asked Julia what is the best thing to do:

HAVING A BREAK FROM SOCIAL MEDIA

JULIA SAMUEL, MBE

I would delete the apps from my phone for that day because why put yourself in the face of danger?
Do things that actively comfort you: buy yourself some flowers, make a nice meal, have a hug from people who love you, get outside, move your body, journal a bit … Do the things that calm you, support you, release you, rather than things that amp up your distress and your pain.

Easier said than done, I know! I try to stay off social media, to enjoy the day and to be present, I really do, but I just find myself looking – it can be a real distraction!

Mother's/Father's Day is really important for stepparents; when you are in a maternal role for a child and looking after them in a motherly way – doing their washing, cooking and taking them to school, for example – it's natural to want some kind of recognition, especially when you've stepped into this role and you're not used to doing all this.

I'm really lucky as Rio was so supportive; we were on the journey together and I felt like I had his full backing. I'm so grateful for that, but I know there are a lot of new stepparents who struggle.

HOW TO SUPPORT A STEPPARENT
PROFESSOR LISA DOODSON

If you are the bio parent, it's really important to recognise your partner for looking after your children. In the early days, it's not what your partner is used to. Give them a hug and tell them they're doing brilliantly. Check they're OK or if there's anything you can do to make things easier. If the children have left, maybe run your partner a bath and tell them to go and relax while you tidy up!

I want to send my love to anyone who is finding things difficult – you are not alone. Mother's/Father's Day is hard. If you are struggling, take a breath, go for a walk, come off social media and surround yourself with people who love you and care for you. The build-up – with the flowers, cards, adverts – can feel overwhelming, but try to remember that it's just another day. Be easy on yourself and cry if you need to – just let it all out.

There is now a National Stepfamily Day, so perhaps that could become a new tradition for your blended family that would make you feel more comfortable with having the focus on you.

However you choose to mark these sometimes difficult days, I'm a great believer that if you don't celebrate yourself, no one else is going to. So celebrate your own accomplishments and feel good about how far you've come, both as a stepparent and as a blended family. Ditch the guilt and become your own champion.

CHAPTER 7

OTHERS AROUND YOU

'Co-parenting is not about asking permission. It's about discussing your child's needs and wants and deciding what's best for them.'

You choose your partner, but you don't choose their previous partner – and just the idea of them can feel challenging. In a child-free relationship, you probably wouldn't discuss past romances, but in a stepfamily, you can't ignore the relationship that produced your stepchildren.

Whether it's the kids' bio parent, extended family members or friends of the bio parent or bereaved family, hopefully you'll get on with them, or at least have a friction-free relationship that is focused on prioritising the kids. Whatever happens, the feelings you have about them, and vice versa, may be tricky, so in this chapter, I want to explore those difficult feelings and give some tips on overcoming imposter syndrome and dealing with preconceptions. I'll also be including a few extra case studies from the Blended community and sharing some expert advice on those scenarios, such as working with the previous partner and dealing with parental alienation, that I don't have experience of.

Being a stepparent is unique in that, all of a sudden, you have to have a relationship with people who don't know you on a personal level, and who you don't know either. You have to communicate with them while you're still learning about each other's characters. This can be very difficult at first and takes some adjustment. Let's be honest, you don't normally have relationships with people you don't really know, but as a stepparent you're thrown into this.

I saw a quote on Instagram recently that said something like, 'If you're not happy with something in your life, change it. If you don't like someone, don't be around them.' In fact, for a lot of my life I lived by this saying … until I became a stepmum! I've realised that life isn't that simple, especially in a blended family. You can't just change something you don't like as it will have a huge effect on the rest of the family. There are going to be people you don't gel with, and you have to put up with them for the children's sake, even if they're not very welcoming.

I'm not just talking about annoying relatives – we all have those! I'm talking about people who disapprove of you because they have fixed ideas of what a family should look like, resent your presence in the children's lives or judge you. Finding a way to manage the situation is difficult when you all see things completely differently.

For me, it's about patience. Change will happen, but there will always be things that remain the same and it's about learning to adapt.

HANDLING DIFFICULT EMOTIONS

In the beginning, I felt a bit like I was living in Rebecca's shadow. I felt that everyone was telling me how I needed to act and that being me wasn't enough. I was so confused; I didn't know what was going on.

In my situation, you can often feel like you're being compared to the previous partner. Everything you do, the previous partner has probably done before, and people may remind you of that, whether they're doing it in a nice way or not. You can feel judged on everything from the way you organise Christmas to how you cook a roast or even plan family days out. If you're feeling sensitive, these emotions can be heightened.

I'd always thought being me was OK, but when I came into this family, I struggled with the idea that I wasn't enough for a really long time. We've come through it now. There's been lots of counselling, lots of therapy, lots of talks with family members, but now I feel confident in my role and we are in a really good place.

Overcoming imposter syndrome

It's not unusual for a stepparent to feel like an outsider at times, and in an earlier chapter, I've looked at how alienating it can feel to join a family that shares memories that don't include you (see page 92). Inevitably, you will hear about moments that you'd rather not know about, like your partner's previous wedding day, or how your stepchildren's bio parents met, or (more likely) where the children were born and in what circumstances. Though these are not your stories, if you think of them as being part of your family's history, they can become yours in a wider sense.

A lot of stepparents feel imposter syndrome. I felt that a lot at the beginning – like I can't get this right, what am I doing wrong, why is this so hard, it should be easier – and sometimes, here and there, I still feel it now, like I'm living

IMPOSTER SYNDROME

im.post.er syn.drome • noun

A psychological state of anxiety, inadequacy, self-doubt or negative self-talk that comes from doubting your own competence, feeling like a fraud and attributing your accomplishments to luck or external factors.

someone else's life and I don't understand how I got here. It just feels strange sometimes.

I spoke to Professor Lisa Doodson about how the early experience can often feel like failure or being an imposter in the family, and how this is really normal. She offered the following tips:

DEALING WITH IMPOSTER SYNDROME
PROFESSOR LISA DOODSON

» First, breathe and relax. It takes time to build a blended family. Don't expect things to happen quickly.

» Read around the topic – go online or read books – just so that it normalises things and you can start to realise that 'it's not just you'.

» Think about what you're really struggling with. Don't try to fix everything at once.

» Work out whether it's you feeling like an imposter or whether it's other people who are making you feel like that.

» Do something that you enjoy – it could be something as simple as just going for a walk.

» Talk. If you're really struggling, reach out to family or friends for support. Sometimes a sympathetic ear is enough to give you a little bit of hope to know that you will start to feel comfortable in your role and it will all be OK in the end. If you need further help, speak to a professional. Try not to let things overwhelm you.

It's OK to be floundering a bit and finding it difficult, but it will get better. It's also OK to reach out.

Family members also experience these feelings in a more typical blended set-up, when the other biological parent is actively involved in the children's lives. It's not necessarily going to be easier or harder than if the previous partner is absent – it's just different if you're dealing with them in person or by text and email. It means that another person is going to influence what happens within your family and their influence will impact anything from the way the children are brought up to your holiday dates. It also means that you, the stepparent, may sometimes be excluded from big decisions about the children's lives, potentially making you feel like an outsider.

You may already be finding it difficult that you're not a part of your family's shared history and memories; now you also have to accept being on the sidelines at times. Add to this the possibility that your stepchildren may worry that accepting you is a betrayal of their other parent. All this means that you're going to need to draw on your resources of patience, compassion and resilience.

Maybe the first step is accepting that the relationship between a biological parent and child is special and can't be replicated. At the same time, although the relationship you have with your stepchild is different from the one they have with their bio parent, it can also be very close and very special. You are lucky to have each other. Although I sometimes struggle with the fact that I'm not the kids' bio parent and haven't known them all their lives, I've tried to change my mindset and be grateful that we have each other. It is such a special bond.

> *I love my son far more than I could ever dislike his stepparent. Although we may not always agree, we both want what's best for him.*
>
> JEN, BLENDED FAMILY OF FIVE

DEALING WITH PRECONCEPTIONS

When Rio and I got together, I know that a lot of people thought, 'They're not going to last. Look at them: ex-footballer, three kids; *TOWIE* girl; no chance!' I think this spurred me on, actually. I knew we were going to last; I was never going to give up.

People on Rio's side of the fence thought he was having a bit of a crisis because he was going out with this silly, young girl – and I'd never to be able to look after his kids. So, while Rio and I were madly in love on one side, on the other side it felt as if we were fighting against the whole world. And I felt I had to prove myself because it seemed to me as if everyone was waiting for me to fail and wanting it to go wrong.

It was really, really difficult for a couple of years, because I was taking on three children with a lot of grief and I needed all the support I could get. I don't really know how we overcame it; I just think we didn't give up and eventually people saw me for who I was. I just continued being me, hoping that people would eventually see that my intentions were good. It's a fine line between not letting people walk all over you and trying to be the bigger person. It's a tricky one and you're not always going to get it right. I bit back a few times when people were horrible to me at first – sometimes you can't help snapping if you feel attacked or criticised – but mostly I tried to hold back. I feel much better about that whole situation because a lot of the relationships have mended.

It is very easy for people on the outside to say, 'Don't worry, it's their problem. They are obviously not happy them-selves; you carry on.' But when it's directed at you all the time, it can be hard to accept it and keep going.

Through all the tough times, difficult conversations, feel-ing judged by certain people … I just tried to remind myself that I have pure intentions and I'm trying to do what's best for the kids. I hoped that, in time, everyone would be able to see that.

As the new partner and stepparent, it's important to remember that other people's hostility and negativity is more about the situation than it is about you. They don't want to see *anybody* taking your position. Change is hard and it takes a while for people to adapt.

Tip: You *can* have happiness after loss and you have to live life to the fullest as you don't know how long you have left.

Julia Samuel told me: 'When you grieve, it opens up your heart to feel love in an even stronger way because you've felt so much sorrow that it opens you up to even more love.' I think that's a really nice way of seeing grief and that there's a form of positivity that comes afterwards.

> *I was 25 when I cared for and lost my husband to a long, awful battle with cancer. We had a beautiful little girl, who was four when her father died.*
>
> *I met my partner two years later and we began to date, and I slowly introduced him to my daughter and my family. My late husband's family were really understanding and have welcomed him into the fold, but a few of my friends were asking questions like, 'Are you sure it's not too soon?' or 'What are you doing?' If they saw us hold hands or hug, they'd almost wince, which felt sad to me because I had grieved so much, even when my husband was alive; my life consisted of caring for him, our daughter and hospital visits, and watching him struggle. I felt like I deserved happiness and nobody else could understand that.*
>
> *My friends suggested I must 'be over' my husband if I had a new partner, which is ridiculous, because you never 'get over' grief. My husband is loved and missed every day; we talk about him and his photos are up in our new home.*

> *My friends are supportive now that they've got to know my partner, so things are much better. He is a superhero! He has taken my daughter on as his own and helps her to navigate grief and the unfair situation she is in. He has always felt comfortable with having photos up. He said that at first he found it strange when we all used to talk about my husband, but he now understands that he's just a big part of our lives; he will comfort me if I'm sad or if my daughter is having a hard time.*
>
> *We are now a blended family of four and there is a lot of joy in our lives. However, there will always be times that are sad and we work through them together.*
>
> JAZ, BLENDED FAMILY OF FOUR

People put us in boxes and they often think you can't come out of that box. Don't believe other people's limitations on you. You can go above that.

WORKING WITH THE PREVIOUS PARTNER

> *'If a mother and father can love more than one child, then why is it so hard to understand that a child can love more than one mother and father?'*

However hard it is to feel like an outsider, I find it helpful to see the three of us as parents and, when it comes to the kids, I do consider what Rebecca would think and whether she'd be happy with what I'm doing. It might sound a bit odd considering I didn't know her, but I like to think of myself in that position and what I would be happy with. As a mum, all I would want if something were to happen to me would be for my children to be safe and happy and loved.

My situation's unique and I know there can sometimes be a lot of tension between bio parents and stepparents.

In an ideal world, every member of the extended family would want to work towards helping the children adjust to the huge changes that are happening in their lives, as a new family (or two) takes shape after a break-up or bereavement. But, unfortunately, it doesn't always happen that way.

> *I always thought it strange that my stepdaughter's mum never wanted to meet me, the woman who was around her daughter every other weekend. I know that would be my first thought if my partner was with another woman. I understand it can't be easy for someone to have their child around another woman, but if she met me, knew me, she would know she 100 per cent has nothing to worry about. 'I've been told I'm not allowed to like you,' my stepdaughter has told me, although who knows who said it or how it was said. I only know that I would never disrespect her mum in front of her and would always promote their relationship.*

DANIELLE, BLENDED FAMILY OF THREE

Letting go of resentments

It's tempting in some instances to feel resentful of the bio parent. You might even feel jealous of them, inadequate or undervalued in comparison, especially if you feel they are being prioritised over you by your partner and stepchildren. This is when it helps to think about your role and what it really means to be a bonus parent.

Being clear about your role will help you draw distinct lines around your responsibilities and obligations and make it easier to say no – or yes – if the bio parent tries to lean on you to do extra chores. For example, they might hand over children with bags full of dirty clothes on transition day, but expect you to hand over to them children with clean clothes. It may sound like a small thing, but week after week, something like this can quickly build into resentment, so it's best to address it as soon as possible and agree a plan.

In many cases, you may not get a lot of thanks from the other bio parent for your efforts to nurture and care for their children. This comes with the territory, unfortunately, or so I'm told by some of the stepparents I've spoken to. Look to your partner for acknowledgement of all that you do – hopefully they will be the one encouraging and appreciating you all the way!

HOW TO AVOID FEELING RESENTFUL
PROFESSOR LISA DOODSON

Most stepparents experience resentment at some point and *all* feel embarrassed or ashamed of their feelings. So if this strikes a chord with you, remember it's normal and common. Your resentment may be directed at the children or, more often, the other bio parent. Try to talk to your partner about how you feel and what you could do together to make some changes.

» If you take on more of the extra household work when the children stay, try to make sure it's not too one-sided. Rope in your partner to help, or even the children. And don't just assume it's your job – work out what you're prepared to do to help your partner when their children are living with you.

» Make sure you make time just for you when the home is full. Perhaps meet a friend for a coffee, go for a walk or just take yourself off to a quiet corner to regroup and recharge your batteries!

» If your resentment is more focused on your partner's ex, you need to try to find a way of limiting their impact on your life.

» If they are constantly imposing themselves – either through frequent calls, emails or messages – try to minimise that, or at least your involvement in them. Make sure all conversations are limited to practical issues rather than emotional.

» Remember that you might not be the children's bio parent, but you are 'the' parent in your home and it's up to you and your partner to set the boundaries and rules for your family life.

Zoe and Toni are two mums with six children between them. Toni is stepmum to Zoe's son, Alfie, and the two families have always had a positive relationship. At the core is a friendship between the two women. How did they achieve this?

While at the start it was polite and easy, we grew as families and so did our friendship. At times, blended family life can be difficult, especially when it means splitting time between two homes and making those tough decisions as children get older. When there is a big decision to be made, or even a situation that has occurred with Alfie, the three of us sit down and run through everything together. While we may not always agree, we always find the best path for Alfie.

I would say that the key is not to push for a friendship, but to be positive role models for your children and take it from there. It also happens that Alfie's father isn't the greatest at communication and that has meant we have relied on each other to relay important information and to provide emotional support. We are very appreciative of how lucky we are. As a mum, all you want is the best for your children and it's made that much easier when you see that the woman who becomes your son's stepmum cares for him as if he were her own, but never wishes to take your place.

We are both quite honest and open with each other. As two mums, we appreciate and understand how the other may feel in certain situations. There is no competition between us to be the better family. What we often do is include us all.

ZOE AND TONI, BLENDED FAMILY OF EIGHT

Agreeing on a parenting plan

Even when everyone's getting on fine, co-parenting can be a minefield of clashing dates and missed information. This is something I don't know much about because it's not my experience and, to be honest, I'd probably try to manage everything on Google Calendar!

I met Ainsley, a proud mum of three, when she was going through a divorce. Soon afterwards, Ainsley joined the Blended team. She's got some great input about how to organise co-parenting:

'As a parent splitting up, I panicked about everything and anything! Who would have the children at Christmas, which days I would have the children, how we would decide on schools, what about holidays ... The list was endless. So when we separated, the best decision we made was our parenting plan to help with co-parenting (we share the children 50:50).

'A parenting plan can be whatever you want it to be and we found an amazing guide and free template on the Cafcass website (see page 218). It really helped us to communicate and write down the best way forward to co-parent successfully.

'We included things like:

» how we would make big decisions about the children

» how we would share special occasions like birthdays

» if we needed to bring in a third party if we couldn't agree on something and who that person would be

'We even talked about introducing new partners and how the dynamics may change. Every detail, including school reports and possible issues, was discussed and agreed upon, and then written down.

'A parenting plan is not a legal document – you can just both sign it and keep it or, as we've done, have it witnessed by our solicitors so that we feel it is a more binding understanding. We will also revisit it as the children get older and situations change. It gives me peace of mind that if anything were to go wrong in the future, I have the document to refer back to and discuss with my ex.

'I know that in some situations it's not possible to do something like this, as one parent may not want to, or it proves difficult to communicate without a mediator of some kind. Some people write them during mediation, showing that both parents have the best interests of the children at heart.'

This sounds like a really sensible idea to me.

COMMUNICATION

Lots of the stepparents I've heard from are challenged by their relationships with the non-resident biological parent of their stepchildren. It's no surprise that sometimes bad feeling will exist between ex-partners and new partners; there's even a term for the difficult other parent that seems to be quite widely used – the 'high-conflict bio mum or dad'.

Even if relations are good between you and your partner and the non-resident parent of your stepkids, intentions can be misunderstood and meanings muddled. Clear communication is so important, but what's the best way to get your message across?

TIPS FOR CONFLICT-FREE COMMUNICATION
LAURA NASER

1. Switch it up. If verbal communication tends to
    end in an argument or being talked over, switch
    to messages or emails so that you can take your
    time to consider what you want to say and make
    sure you have said all you want to cover. Carefully
    consider the tone, which can only be inferred
    in written communications. This way all major
    communications will also be documented between
    you, which will reduce any misunderstandings and
    might serve as evidence should you later need it.
    Remember to back up those messages!

2. Try to remove emotion from your messages, although
    I appreciate that this is far more easily said than
    done. I encourage my clients to write out their initial
    sparky responses but never press send. Instead, I ask
    to save them into a file or send them to a best friend
    for a bit of cathartic release.

3. Set boundaries. Keep communications to business
    hours, unless in an emergency. Only engage
    in communication in a particular way, such as
    WhatsApp or email, except to allow phone calls in
    an emergency or to facilitate a child speaking to the
    other parent. Only read messages at set times or days
    of the week. These can be great techniques if, for
    example, you find there is a pattern with arguments
    tending to arise in the evenings, or where you find
    the correspondence is impacting upon your ability

to do your job or relax and switch off in an evening. You can set up rules in your email inbox to put emails into a separate file so that you only read them at a set time of the day, and don't respond for at least 24 hours. You can also mute a WhatsApp chat, which gives you a similar uninterrupted control over receiving messages.

4. Sometimes picking up the phone or a face-to-face talk might help to press the reset button. This is not going to be appropriate for all co-parents, but for some the back and forth on messages and the anxiety and misunderstandings it can cause can be quickly addressed and calmed by talking to each other. You can start this with something along the lines of: 'This isn't going as I had hoped it would for us and I want us to do better, so can we talk about it and get in a better place please?'

Tip: **I'm the sort of person who likes to be involved in everything. I like to know what the kids are up to when they go to stay with other people in the family. Something that's worked for us is setting up a WhatsApp group to exchange photos so that everyone feels involved. That way everyone gets to share in the kids' experiences.**

DRAWING UP A CONTACT AGREEMENT
LAURA NASER

If you've been trying but finding making arrangements and communication difficult, which can often happen if there's hostility between you and your co-parent, or where you don't have a shared opinion of what's best for the child, it might be a good idea to agree on some ground rules when it comes to having contact with one another and for your arrangements for the children. A way forward can be to draw up an agreement, because sometimes tempers can fray …

The agreement is not legally binding, so there aren't any immediate consequences for failing to uphold your agreed terms, and it won't give any authorities (such as the school or the police) any ability to assist you in upholding the agreed terms either. However, it does set the framework for your joint intentions, and any significant or repeated breaches could be relied upon later, should matters deteriorate and you have to use the courts, to support what changes you might seek to the arrangements for your children as a consequence.

Here's an example of how the agreement could look:

Respect

»   To be polite in our dealings with one another and try never to shout.

»   To keep disagreements and conflict away from the children – out of sight and out of hearing.

» To hold back from criticising each other in front of or within earshot of the children, and to not allow others to do so either.

Communication

» To agree on our lines of communication, how often we will be in contact and the issues we'll be liaising about.

» To respond within an appropriate timeframe to queries.

» To share any concerns we have about the children's mental or physical health and agree on a strategy to help them.

» To try to see things from the other person's point of view and not overstep the mark in our discussions.

Arrangements

» To stick to agreed arrangements, especially timings.

» To make transitions or handovers as smooth as possible for the children.

» To give each other as much notice as possible should either of us request any adjustments to the arrangements.

» To make arrangements with the children's best interests as our primary focus when making these decisions.

Trust

» To listen to each other's opinions with a sense of trust, rather than suspicion, and with a willingness to understand.

» To be honest in our interactions.

» To be kind and fair in our communications which will help to rebuild any damaged trust.

Compromise

» To be prepared to meet halfway when we can't reach an agreement.

» To work together to achieve a shared goal.

» To have an agreed way forward if agreement cannot be reached, such as to attend mediation or to arbitrate the issue.

If you're dealing with a high-conflict situation, it may be difficult or impossible to make a contact agreement like this between you and the other biological parent. If you're really struggling, please seek professional support.

When I met my late husband, George, he was recently divorced; he had three young children and shared custody of them with his ex-wife. When I moved in with him, the children were living primarily with their mum.

Two years later, due to changes in circumstances, the children came back to live with us, which was a significant adjustment for everyone involved. However, the children settled in school and everyone got used to their new routine. George and I married in my home country, Uganda, with the children in tow.

The first few years were difficult as the co-parenting relationship between the children's mum and my husband was strained. New to the family, this complex relationship was difficult for me to navigate. I loved the children like they were my own, which became a point of contention between me and their mum, and for years our relationship was a challenging one.

Unfortunately, my husband became chronically ill and was also made redundant from his job, which made me the main breadwinner. I worked all hours to ensure that the family was provided for and that we were able to keep a roof over our heads.

When my husband passed, the whole family was devastated by his loss. The following years were some of the most challenging of my life. Without the support of my late husband, it was significantly more difficult to navigate the co-parenting relationship with his ex-wife. We went for long periods without any communication and then got into heated disagreements, which severed all hopes for a positive co-parenting relationship going forward. My stepdaughter stayed with me after her dad's passing and I worked hard to provide for us and to ensure that we did not lose the family house.

A few years later, I met my current partner and over the years he has developed his own relationship with each of my stepchildren, with whom I remain as close as ever.

*Surprisingly, in recent times, my relationship with the
children's mum has improved greatly to the point that I
would now consider her a friend. When my stepdaughter
graduated from university, her mum, my partner, her
brother and I were all in attendance. Since then, we
have celebrated the children's birthdays together as a
family. Years ago, this would never have seemed possible
and there were many times when I felt like giving up,
but if I had, I would have missed out on these beautiful
relationships, so I'm glad that I had the foresight to look
at the bigger picture.*

FLAVIA, STEPMUM OF THREE

THE UNRELIABLE PARENT

Of course you're going to feel annoyed if the children's other
parent doesn't turn up or call as arranged, leaving your stepchild feeling hurt, confused or worried. Seeing a child upset
is hard and you're the one who has to pick up the pieces.
I've heard from several stepparents in the Blended community who've been impacted by a bio parent's indifference,
and from others about how they've had to deal with absence
caused by chaos and addiction. Here are some of their tips
for dealing with this:

> » Allow your stepchild to let out their feelings after
> they've been let down or disappointed. Sit with them
> in their pain.

> » Emphasise that it is not their fault, without criticising
> their parent. Tell them that they are loved and deserve
> to be loved.

» Explain in age-appropriate terms why the parent is absent or unable to keep their promises.

» Point out to them their strengths and talents and try to shift their focus to the things they achieve apart from the parent. Stress that their success and happiness does not depend on that parent.

» Try to stay calm if they get angry. Practise compassion and empathy with them and reassure them of their family's love.

» Manage their expectations before the next potential disappointment in the kindest possible way.

I can only imagine how difficult it must be to be in this situation and my heart goes out to you if you're trying to deal with this. Every child deserves to feel loved and respected.

PARENTAL ALIENATION

Parental alienation is where one parent turns the children against the other parent. It usually happens during or after a messy divorce, but can take place while a marriage is still ongoing. It may also be a problem when stepfamilies break up and a biological parent won't allow an ex-stepparent access to the children, even if they have been a parent figure for many years. Obviously, this can be heartbreaking.

The alienating parent uses lies and negativity to condition the children to keep their distance from – or actively hate – the targeted parent. Reconnecting with children who have been conditioned to hate you is really difficult, especially if the alienating parent has said you left the marriage because you didn't love them.

HOW TO COUNTERACT ATTEMPTS AT PARENTAL ALIENATION

LAURA NASER

The source of genuine parental alienation is from the 'influencing parent' consciously or subconsciously allowing their animosity and negative opinion of the other parent to influence the child against them to such an extreme extent that the child rejects what was their normal relationship with them.

Parental alienation as a term is quite commonly used, but the true cases are fairly rare, because they really are very extreme situations. It is a form of psychological abuse and if a court does find that parental alienation has taken place, it can result in the children being removed from the 'influencing parent's' care entirely.

Be careful about alleging alienation and in what terms. The phrase is one that I think is often overused, and will no doubt be like throwing a grenade at the other parent, which is ultimately going to make matters worse. Take legal advice as soon as you suspect it is happening so a close eye can be kept on the issues and addressed in a more formal context through your lawyer, and a strategy can be put in place for your options should it carry on. Reacting appropriately and swiftly can make a big difference.

What I say to my clients who suspect the other parent of behaving in a way which might lead to parental alienation is to keep a detailed diary contemporaneous to events, noting exactly what was said and by whom, and what happened, as precisely as possible. It will be difficult for you to remember in a few months' or a year's time exactly how things occurred on any specific occasion, so your diary will act as an accurate record of what you witnessed.

Consider whether it would be helpful to invite your child and/or the other parent to attend therapy together with you. Family therapy or therapy for co-parents might assist in addressing what the issues are and allow you to tackle them with the benefit of professional help.

Through whatever circumstances you come into a bended family, there are going to be ups and downs – and we all hit rocky patches. This quote sums everything up for me:

'When tough times come your way, you really only have two options. You can either fight the waves or you can ride them. You can spend all of your energy wishing things were different and wishing that situations and people would change. You can spend your precious time fighting against reality and all that is – or you can let go and ride the waves. You can soften. You can accept that life brings waves, *and some waves will be undoubtedly wonderful but others will be incredibly tough. My lovely friend, I hope you learn to ride your waves.'*

NIKKI BANAS, AUTHOR

If you're worried about other people's disapproval, remind yourself society is changing and some people adjust and adapt quicker than others. It may sound obvious, but it helps if you can be the change you want to see. If you can do that – if you can be true to yourself and to your stepfamily – the rest will follow.

CHAPTER 8

BEING YOU

'No one is you, and that is your power.'

My whole life changed when I moved in with Rio and the children. I went from partying every weekend to looking after three children aged six, eight and ten. I went from wearing a nice bikini at a beach club to getting drenched in a pool, wearing goggles and yelling, 'Who can do the most lengths underwater?'

I heard from another stepmum who did a similar 180 when she met her partner: 'We became a blended family when I was just 24 years old; my partner's little boy had just turned three at the time,' she says. 'My evenings and weekends shifted from dressing up and going for cocktails to family trips to the zoo and learning the names of all the dinosaurs in the Jurassic period (there are a lot!). Back then I didn't realise how much my partner and his dinosaur-obsessed little boy would change my life forever.'

It's a massive change. All of a sudden I wasn't available to my friends and, even when I did go out, for a really long time I couldn't enjoy myself because I felt so stressed with everything that was going on. So I'd be out, but I wouldn't really be having any fun and couldn't talk to anyone about it. I found myself in this weird situation where people were saying, 'I'm so gutted I couldn't get the outfit I wanted for this event,' and I was listening to them, thinking, 'I'm worlds away from this.'

I felt that no one could understand the issues I was dealing with, especially the children's grief. It was consuming me. I couldn't see through the fog. I felt like I was drowning and, eventually, I pulled back from everyone and threw myself into the family. Something always has to give; life can't be perfect. It's actually a relief when you realise that.

I loved my life with Rio and the children, but I sometimes missed my old life. I was very carefree before I had kids and then I had all this responsibility. It's something every parent feels from time to time, but for me it happened very suddenly.

I know how hard it is in those early days, which is why I wanted to include this chapter in the book and bring the focus back to you – outlining all those self-care tips that we all know we should be doing but struggle to implement in real life.

Tip: **Rio says I don't give myself enough credit, but it's easy to lose yourself in the mix sometimes. Whatever your role, if you run into obstacles, keep reminding yourself how fantastic it is for the children to have an adult in their lives who loves their mum or dad and cares deeply about their well-being and progress. I believe that children can never have too much love or too many loving older figures around.**

BE GOOD TO YOURSELF

This was a difficult section for me to write because I am not very good at following my own advice, but here goes …

Take some time out

You might have heard me say that I enjoy being away from my kids … Just to be clear, I love being with my kids – I love spending quality time with them and doing everything with them – but it's really important for me to also get that time away, for work and for me. When I manage it, I come back to the family with a fresh head and I don't always prioritise that time enough.

You need to make time for yourself – just ten minutes of alone time to sit and be, and not think or stress about anything. This is much easier said than done because, as a parent, you always land at the bottom of the pile. For me, the best thing is going for a walk. Getting fresh air really clears your mind. It is such a simple thing, but I usually feel much better when I come back from a walk. Having a nice warm shower in the evening also gives me that space away from the kids and I can just clear my mind.

Embrace the giggles

It's a massive cliché, but it's true: laughter is the best medicine. Laughter triggers emotional and physical changes in the body by releasing happy chemicals that reduce stress, boost immunity, counteract depression and raise self-esteem and energy levels.

Even though things can be difficult at times, our house is full of so much laughter. There is singing and dancing and football and cartwheels. We're always laughing, even if it's just when we're taking the mickey out of each other. I'm so grateful for the laughs – they make all the hard times so much easier.

Let the tears flow

Conversely, having a cry can also be an amazing emotional release. As I posted on Blended, 'Do not be afraid of crying, especially in front of your children. If our children never see us cry, how will they know that crying is a normal part of life?'

Children need to see you upset, tired, hangry, really happy – all these different emotions. It's just so important for them to see all aspects and all angles of us.

Often we are taught from a young age to hold back our emotions, not to cry, that crying is 'for babies', but we do actually feel much lighter once we have had a good cry. It's a positive thing to express your feelings, as doing so will release oxytocin and endorphins that can help with your emotional pain. Crying is not a sign of weakness. In fact, it shows strength and is part of the overall healing journey.

I wear my heart on my sleeve and the kids either see me dancing around the kitchen or getting emotional watching a film. I pride myself on being open and honest when emotions get on top of me.

Let go of negativity

If your inner voice is telling you that you don't deserve happiness, or that you're not good enough, or not loveable enough, it will become difficult to navigate blended family life with clear eyes. This negative thinking can cloud your judgement and make you feel as though any negativity is aimed at you, when actually it isn't.

I have been guilty of getting caught up in negative self-talk. It's really unhelpful but, when you're in it, you can't stop. Try the following tips to turn this around:

CHALLENGING THE CRITICAL VOICE IN YOUR HEAD

ANNA MATHUR

»   Begin to notice the way you speak to yourself. What kind of words does your self-talk use, what tone does it take? Is it impatient, perfectionist or critical?

»   Consider where your negative self-talk may have come from. Our self-talk can be shaped by many different influences along the way, including how caregivers and pertinent people in our lives have spoken to us and made us feel.

»   Know the costs of continuing this critical self-talk. Think about how your child or friend would feel if you spoke to them in the way that you speak to yourself. Now reflect on how your negative self-talk might have influenced how you feel about and treat yourself over time. The more we recognise how something impacts us, the more motivation we have to change it.

»   Nurture a new way of talking to yourself. When you become aware of your negative self-talk, think about how you might respond to it with some kindness, patience and compassion. Consider how you'd speak to your child or friend if they uttered these negative words to you. Patience and kindness nurture self-esteem and confidence, and bring important balance to negative or critical self-talk.

» Keep on keeping on. Addressing self-talk isn't about eradicating all negative or critical thoughts, but just bringing some balance to them so that they aren't the only and loudest voice in your mind. Be patient with yourself, and instead of trying to change it overnight, opt for a 'more of the time, not all of the time' approach.

My therapist advised me to consider how much I was talking about the negative experiences I was having with my blended family and with my husband's ex-wife. I didn't realise it myself, but by continually talking about the bad experiences, the negative feelings were taking over and defining me and how I was feeling day to day. Once I was aware of this, I was more careful about what I was saying, and to whom. I'm naturally a very sunshiny, positive, glass-very-full person! I realised that my self-talk, and how I spoke to others, wasn't making my usual disposition very achievable, and I didn't want to feel upset all the time.

CHLOE, MUM OF TWO, STEPMUM OF THREE

Tip: **You are where you are now – and so is your partner, and so is their ex, and so are the children. For better or worse, the past cannot be changed, so keep hoping and believing in the future.**

Check in with your feelings

Emotions are at the core of everything we think, say and do, and there are plenty of them bouncing around as parents and children tackle the challenges of building a new family structure.

Things can get really mixed up when life gets complicated – and being in touch with your emotional responses is a key part of staying balanced and calm as you deal with the bumps and potholes in the road ahead.

Identifying your feelings is key to dealing with them:

» Once you've pinpointed them, try to find a calm way of expressing them.

» Sit with your feelings and gently detach yourself from them by remembering that other stepparents have experienced and worked through similar issues, situations and emotions.

» Make sure you don't act out of rage.

» Talk to a friend – ideally someone who understands.

» If the children have said something hurtful, remind yourself that they are still developing their consciousness and are often unaware of their impact on others. Put yourself in their shoes.

» Let compassion in – for yourself as well as others around you.

PRIORITISE YOUR MENTAL WELL-BEING

Making sure you look after your mental health is one of the most important things you can do, not only for yourself but for your family too. Just because you can't see it, doesn't mean it's not there. Our mental health is often overlooked because of how we visually look from the outside.

Surround yourself with people who care

If therapy isn't available to you, for whatever reason, it can help to just speak to your partner or your friends – just sharing a problem can often be enough. It takes a weight off your shoulders. It works wonders for your sense of self to spend time with friends who love you – especially people who knew you before you became a stepparent and can remind you of who you are and how loved you are. I've got a few really good friends from my past who I cherish.

Talking things through with your partner can really help, but sometimes having a friendly ear outside the home is also useful. With a friend you are able to be completely honest about your insecurities when it comes to being a stepparent, and how that impacts your relationship.

However, in the early days I spoke to my family and friends, but I felt like they didn't really understand, so that made me feel even more alone and I felt a bit isolated. As with any situation, you sometimes don't appreciate something fully until you've gone through it yourself. So, as much as your friends and family may want to try to understand and talking to them can be a release because they know and love you, they may not be able to relate to your situation. A lot of people in more conventional family types still don't understand the dynamics of blending.

Find support online

This is where the Blended community really comes into its own. There are forums on the Blended website where you can share your problems and people in a similar situation can give advice and help. This is a safe space for us all to share our blended family experiences and support each other along the way. Here, you can seek out other stepparents who have been through many of the things you have – it can be a real support to just vent sometimes. In the beginning, I didn't realise how important it was to reach out and relate to others going through the same experience, but it really takes a weight off your shoulders. You can also listen to experts giving advice on the *Blended* podcast.

Something I'm so proud of is creating a space for others to speak and be heard without the hefty price tag that sometimes comes with therapy.

That said ...

Try therapy, if you can

Being a stepparent often involves accepting that you're in a situation where not everyone is going to love you and like you. It's easy to think it's your fault, but it might just be the situation you're in. Talking about this to the people who love you and care about you can work wonders, but sometimes you need an expert view.

Picking apart what's going on in your mind can be quite confusing and I've never made a secret of the fact that therapy has helped me over the years. As I'm always saying, if our hair needs doing, we go to the hairdresser. If we fall over and break our arm, we go to the hospital. If our car needs servicing, we take it to the garage ... So why would we not go to someone to help with our internal thoughts and feelings?

Therapy has been in my life for years. It's not something I do all the time, but I know it's there for me to fall back on if

I feel I need that extra help, support, advice or just someone to help me understand what's going on in my head.

All emotions, positive or negative, are valid. If you'd like to minimise their negative effects, it can help to look at what is setting them off. Family dynamics are never straightforward. Our childhoods really do shape us and I'm a great believer that how we were brought up – whether our parents were present or absent – shapes us into the people and the parents that we become. I know I have certain triggers from my childhood and the early years of becoming a stepparent that will set me off. For instance, I felt very alone as a child because I had no siblings and my parents were divorced, and this could be why it's so intense for me when I feel excluded. Recognising this really helps to take the sting out of negative feelings. After all, I'm not that lonely child any more. I'm part of a happy blended family.

Sometimes an emotional trigger is what it is – for instance, you see a photo of a loved one who has passed and feel sad. Other times, you can trace a trigger back to an unhappy experience in childhood. Sometimes triggers can catch me when I least expect it. I've found it helps if I can acknowledge what has set me off and talk about it with Rio, and potentially the older children, so they can understand why I'm reacting the way I am. It also helps me to recognise those triggers when they come up again, so I can manage them before I react in the wrong way.

Try to be honest with yourself when big feelings come up. Though it's hard, it's about learning about yourself so you can be the best stepparent you can be. If you have more complex childhood traumas or are experiencing anxiety, stress, low mood or panic and finding it hard to cope with everyday life, please seek out professional help (see pages 211–12). Therapy, also known as counselling, can often help and is a confidential process of exploring feelings, behaviour and issues that are causing you problems. These problems could include anything that is getting in the way of normal, healthy and happy functioning in everyday life, from your relationships to self-image and self-esteem.

WHAT TO EXPECT WHEN YOU SEE A COUNSELLOR
SOPHIE RANTZAU

When you see a counsellor, they'll have an objective view. They will also be able to help you understand what's going on for you. A counsellor can have a different perspective and be curious about things that haven't occurred to you.

Sometimes when we're in the midst of it, we don't notice the slight changes, or the small wins, or whatever it might be that could be moving us forward.

I first started to experience anxiety when I became a stepmum. I tried to push my feelings aside and get on with my daily life, but it was impossible. The anxiety built and built daily for about six months: I was barely sleeping and couldn't think about anything other than the way I was feeling – and how I was going to get through the next hour, never mind the day! I became forgetful, was barely functioning at work and cried more than I care to remember; I felt like a zombie trudging around stuck in my own head and tried my best to exclude myself from the people who cared about me the most.

Eventually, I got to a point where I had to reach out and get some help. I remember sitting at the kitchen table one morning before school, looking at the children having their breakfast and thinking, 'How am I supposed to look after them, if I can't even function myself?' I will never forget how awful, low and sad I felt in that moment. I felt I had failed as a partner, a mother and a stepmother. This was the moment I knew I needed to do something. I went to my GP, explained my situation and they recommended I go to therapy.

I organised therapy and went religiously every week for 14 months. My recovery was very slow and gradual. I learned in therapy that I needed to take care of myself first and if I didn't do that, I was no good to anybody else.

Eventually, I started to see the light, thanks to more self-care and a combination of therapy, exercising and eating well. I still get bouts of anxiety, but I can manage them now. Anxiety is my body's way of telling me that I need to slow down, take a step back and go back to basics – and that's the best advice I ever received.

SIOBHAN, MUM OF ONE, STEPMUM OF TWO

Where to get help

If you're struggling mentally, the first thing to remember is that you are not alone. Secondly, try to decide how much help you need and want, from self-maintenance to having one-to-one therapy with an expert (see page 219 for resources to help with this).

You can now access the NHS talking therapies service without a referral from your GP (you refer yourself online) or a GP can refer you. These services include counselling, CBT and guided self-help.

Some of the targeted therapies that might be of particular benefit to members of stepfamilies are:

» family therapy (understanding family dynamics and communication)

» couples therapy (for problems within partnerships)

» psychodynamic psychotherapy (exploring childhood and the subconscious)

» interpersonal therapy (looking at all relationships and ways of relating)

If there's a long waiting list or you would prefer to access a private service, ask your GP or a trusted friend for a recommendation for local therapists. Some counsellors work on a payment sliding scale, allowing their clients to pay what they can afford. Or try online therapy in the interim. See page 219 for more resources.

LOOK TO THE FUTURE

It's a relief when you feel you're in a more stable place as a stepfamily. Now it's not about putting out fires; things are running more smoothly and it feels like you've all made space for each other in the family. The household has a rhythm and, as the stepparent, you know what you're doing – most of the time!

Perhaps you feel left out at times; perhaps you wish you didn't have to explain how your family fits together every time you meet someone new. You may still have occasional moments when you wish you'd settled down with someone who didn't already have children or feel sad that your divorce led to the break-up of your first family. But mostly you'll be happy that you put in the effort and things are working out.

It's great to feel that you and your stepchildren are getting on and that you and your partner are united as you navigate a path through blending and parenting, and your love for each other is as strong as ever, or stronger. Hopefully the kids are getting on with each other too.

The challenges of building a new family structure are constantly shifting and changing, but if you've worked hard on the foundations, and patience and compassion are built into the family framework, life is going to be a lot easier from now on. That's not to say that there won't be storms and rainy days ahead. No family can avoid these, blended or not. But being a stepparent and shaping your new family together can be incredibly rewarding.

Here are a few tips for keeping a happy balance going forward:

» Hold on to empathy.

» Stay connected.

» Keep listening.

» Pick your battles.

» Keep laughing.

» Be grateful.

» Look after yourself.

» Enjoy your partner.

» Give yourself a pat on the back.

And remember ... love is the key to everything. For me, especially in our house, as long as we have that foundation of love, we can thrive in other ways. Whatever we are going through individually, or as a family, our love binds us together.

FINAL WORD

'Blended families are woven together by choice, strengthened by love, tested by everything and each is uniquely ours.'

ANONYMOUS

We've come to the end of the book! As I'm sitting here, writing these final words, I've realised how many emotions this book has brought up and I'm only recognising now, looking back, how far I've come. As I've been writing this book, I've been in tears thinking about how much of a fragile space I was in in those early days and how I was desperately trying to please everyone. I'm really proud of where I am now, the way I view myself and how I've grown as a person, but I'm also proud of keeping at it and working hard to form our blended family unit. Don't get me wrong, it's still hard sometimes, and at times I can still feel like an outsider, which brings up so many emotions – and there are still moments of grief and sadness. It's hard and it's sad and it's been a journey, but overall we are a happy, imperfect family.

If you are earlier in your stepparenting journey than I am, I hope that this book has helped you get through the tough times and given you some hope that, with time, everything will fall into place.

There's no doubt that stepparenting *is* all about the children, but always remember you only have one life and you have to try to find the joy, even if it's within the small things.

It's OK to be sensitive – you're only human and emotions will sometimes get the better of you ... but don't let the bad days and the bad moments define who you are as a stepparent.

When I think about it, my whole family is formed from the love that Rio and I have for one another. I count myself lucky – this is the love I've always dreamed of. I always try to remind myself of that when times are hard. Never underestimate what you and your partner are doing here. Love is one of the most powerful emotions of all. But not everyone finds it. Take strength from the fact that you and your partner have each other.

You've got this.

RESOURCES

BLENDED

To become part of the Blended community, follow @blended on Instagram and listen to the podcast.

WHERE TO GET HELP

Access and custody

For information on making child arrangements, go to the **government** website (www.gov.uk/looking-after-children-divorce) as well as **Citizens Advice** (www.citizens advice.org.uk/family/making-agreements-about-your-children/making-child-arrangements). Websites such as https://rightsofwomen.org.uk/ and www.familylawgroup.co. uk also have useful information.

Adoption

For advice on adoption, start by heading to the **government** website (www.gov.uk/government/publications/adoption-statutory-guidance-2013), contact the charity **Adoption UK** (www.adoptionuk.org) or **Barnardo's** (www.barnardos.org. uk), or chat to a local charity near you.

Bereavement

If you'd like to find out more about how children feel and react when they are grieving, **Child Bereavement UK** (www.childbereavementuk.org) has a lot of helpful information on their website.

Grief Encounter (www.griefencounter.org.uk) is another charity offering support to bereaved children and young people, and it has produced a series of helpful grief guides.

Co-parenting

The Children and Family Court Advisory and Support Service, more commonly known as 'CAFCASS', have a useful guide on their website for a parenting plan that includes a downloadable template of some questions for co-parents to discuss along with sections for you to document your agreements. It is available via www.cafcass.gov.uk.

Another useful resource is **Resolution**'s website pages 'Parenting Through Separation'. Resolution is an organisation of 6,500 family law professionals, and its resources can be accessed at www.resolution.org.uk.

Fostering

To find out more about foster care, foster initiatives and fostering in general, please contact your local authority, or get in touch with some charities in this space: **The Fostering Network** (www.thefosteringnetwork.org.uk) and **Barnardo's** (www.barnardos.org.uk).

Mental health support

For advice on how to look after your mental health, including tips on sleep, self-care and dealing with money worries, try the **Every Mind Matters** website (www.nhs.uk/every-mind-matters/).

The mental health charity **Mind** (www.mind.org) has a wealth of resources about mental health issues and how to get help if you need it.

USEFUL APPS

Mental health apps

Thrive, **Headspace** and **Beat Panic** can teach you coping skills. **Chill Panda** is great for breathing exercises; **WorryTree** helps you think through your cares and concerns using an interactive journal and cognitive behavioural therapy (CBT); and **My Possible Self** features a mood tracker, among other brilliant tools.

It's quite a crowded marketplace and many of mental health apps are free to download, so the chances are you'll be able to find one that suits your needs.

Organisational apps

Lists To Do, **24Me**, **Actions by Moleskine**, **Any.do** and **Evernote** are among the apps available for managing lists, notes, event reminders and bills. Ask friends for app recommendations and choose the one with the interface that appeals most.

Cozi Family Organiser is a simple and free family management app that logs family and individual events so that everybody knows what everyone else is doing. **Family Wall** is another good organiser, with a shared calendar, shopping lists and messaging.

Focus is a time-management app that divides your working day into chunks, with regular breaks and a task tracker for anything from housework to homework. **Toggl** shows you how much time you're spending on different tasks, to help you manage time better.

Kitche is a useful app for meal planning, especially if you're the type of person who forgets what you've bought. Scan in your shopping receipts and it can suggest meal ideas and let you know sell-by dates. There are also apps for managing your fridge (**MyFridge**) and avoiding waste (**NoWaste**).

Co-parenting apps

AppClose is a parenting app with a multifunctional shared calendar and templates for parenting schedules, plus more – and it's free.

Our Family Wizard, a US app that's very popular in the UK, offers shared calendars, messages, photos, files, contacts and expense sheets, at a glance.

2Houses offers shared calendars, a journal and photos, along with easily accessible school info and medical files, saving you hours of scrolling through emails and messages for notes and details.

Talking Parents has a shared calendar and secure, unalterable messaging between parents (very useful if there is ever conflict over what has been agreed).

Also check out: **Custody Connection**, **FamCal** and **WeParent**.

FURTHER READING

Allen, Louise, *How to Adopt a Child* (Vermilion, 2021)

Doodson, Lisa, *How to Be a Happy Stepmum* (Vermilion, 2010)

Hindmarch, Anya, *If in Doubt, Wash Your Hair* (Bloomsbury Publishing, 2022)

Keogh, Abel, *Life with a Widower* (Ben Lomond Press, 2013)

Keogh, Abel, *Marrying a Widower* (Ben Lomond Press, 2012)

Knight, Sarah, *The Life-Changing Magic of Not Giving a F**k* (Quercus, 2015)

Martin, Wednesday, *Stepmonster* (CreateSpace Independent Publishing Platform, 2015)

Mathur, Anna, *Know Your Worth* (Piatkus, 2021)

Nafousi, Roxie, *Manifest* (Michael Joseph, 2022)

Naser, Laura, *The Family Lawyer's Guide to Separation and Divorce* (Vermilion, 2019)

Rantzau, Sophie, *When Families End and Blend* (Sophie Rantzau, 2021)

Samuel, Julia, *Every Family Has a Story* (Penguin Life, 2022)

Samuel, Julia, *Grief Works* (Penguin Life, 2018)

Smith, Julie, *Why Has Nobody Told Me This Before?* (Michael Joseph, 2022)

Svanberg, Emma, *Parenting for Humans* (Vermilion, 2023)

Thompson, Dominique, and Vailes, Fabienne, *How to Grow a Grown Up* (Vermilion, 2019)

ACKNOWLEDGEMENTS

To Rio, my world. I couldn't do life without you.

To Lorenz, Tate, Tia and Cree, my crazy kids. You've brought so much joy and happiness to my life. I love you all so much.

To my family, thanks for loving and accepting me for me.

To Nadia and Gemma, and the team at Mokkingbird, thank you for the constant support and always being there for me.

To Julia, thanks for supporting me through this and for all the hours of talking, tears and laughter.

To Sam, Rebecca and all the team at Ebury, thanks for all your patience and helping bring my vision to life.

To the Blended community, thank you for letting me tell my story without judgement and for sharing your ups and downs along the way.

To Ryan, Megan and Faith, and the team at Mags Creative, thank you for always encouraging me and helping me feel confident in speaking my truth.

To all the people who support me on a daily basis – you know who you are! I couldn't do what I do without your constant love, guidance and support.

To Rebecca, thank you for raising three beautiful children; it's a privilege to look after them. We know you are guiding us on our journey.

INDEX

Note: page numbers in **bold** refer to charts and illustrations.